CRITICAL STUDIES OF
KEY TEXTS

Jane Austen's
Sense and Sensibility

D1553172

Other titles available in the series

Liz Bellamy
Jonathan Swift's Gulliver's Travels

Nicola Bradbury
Charles Dickens' Great Expectations

David Fuller
James Joyce's Ulysses

Pauline Nestor
Charlotte Brontë's Jane Eyre

Susanne Raitt
Virginia Woolf's To the Lighthouse

David Seed
James Joyce's A Portrait of the Artist as a Young Man

T. R. Wright
George Eliot's Middlemarch

By the same author

*The Age of William Wordsworth: Critical essays on the Romantic
   tradition* (edited with Kenneth R. Johnston, 1987)

*Wordsworth and Coleridge: The making of the major lyrics, 1802–
   1804* (1989)

The Romantics and Us: Essays on literature and culture (1990)

CRITICAL STUDIES OF
KEY TEXTS

Jane Austen's
Sense and Sensibility

Gene W. Ruoff

St. Martin's Press
New York

AAZ7565

First published in the United States of America in 1992

Printed in Great Britain

ISBN 0–312–08424–2 (cloth)
ISBN 0–312–08599–0 (pbk)

Library of Congress Cataloging-in-Publication Data
Ruoff, Gene W.
    Jane Austen's Sense and sensibility / Gene W. Ruoff.
        p.   cm. – (Critical studies of key texts)
    Includes bibliographical references and index.
    ISBN 0–312–08424–2 (cloth). – ISBN 0–312–08599–0 (paper)
    1. Austen, Jane. 1775–1817. Sense and sensibility.   I. Title.
    II. Series.
    PR4034.S43R86   1992
    823'.7—dc20   92–17361
                                                         CIP

Contents

Note on the Texts

All references to Jane Austen's novels are to the following editions:

The Novels of Jane Austen. Edited by R. W. Chapman. 5 vols. 3rd edn. London: Oxford University Press, 1932–4. The standard scholarly edition. *Sense and Sensibility* is Volume 1, cited parenthetically throughout. References to Austen's other novels are cited parenthetically by volume number (2–5).

Minor Works. Edited by R. W. Chapman. Vol. VI of *Novels of Jane Austen*. London: Oxford University Press, 1954. Cited parenthetically in this study as Volume 6 of the novels.

References to critical works and other sources are also given parenthetically in the text and included in the bibliography.

Acknowledgements

A sabbatical leave from the University of Illinois at Chicago provided me with time to write this study. Its numerous debts to generations of Jane Austen scholars and critics are, I hope, duly noted. Particular debts are gratefully acknowledged to Karl Kroeber, over whose shoulder I first read Austen; to Jim Chandler, who made me read Burke and Paine; to Claudia L. Johnson, who gave me the benefit of a close, perceptive, and enriching reading of my reading; and to Anthony Gregg Roeber, who has helped me through the maze of English inheritance law.

Some material adapted from my previous essays on Austen published in *The Wordsworth Circle* has found its way into this study. I am grateful to Marilyn Gaull for permission to include it here.

Preface

Sense and Sensibility is probably the least familiar and certainly the least fully studied of the four novels Jane Austen published in her lifetime. I have chosen to write on it for one paramount reason: novelists' first published works are normally crucial to understanding their subsequent development. During her correction of the proofsheets in 1811, Austen remarked of the novel to her sister Cassandra, 'I can no more forget it, than a mother can forget her sucking child' (*Letters* 272). Because *Sense and Sensibility* is a book which has much to say about the metaphor of birth and especially birth-order, turning as it does on economic questions of primogeniture and patrilinearity, the many dodges through which commentators have evaded the novel's own primacy are themselves a part of its interesting cultural history.

Critics commonly rehistoricise Austen's canon to place the posthumously-published *Northanger Abbey* first in order, on the grounds that an early version of this gothic parody was actually sold to a publisher in 1803. Less frequently they award priority to *Pride and Prejudice*, because an early version of it was offered for publication and rejected in 1797. Some of the very best criticism has been even more adventurous in its search for a starting-point for consideration of the author: Alistair Duckworth's *The Improvement of the Estate* (1971) begins with a detailed reading of *Mansfield Park*, first published in 1814, as the work which epitomises Austen's mature philosophy, and goes on to treat the earlier work as proleptic to what is for Duckworth Austen's masterpiece; Susan Morgan's

In the Meantime (1980) divides the canon into novels of crisis and novels of passage and begins with the former, starting with *Emma*, which came out in late 1815 (dated 1816), a year and a half before the author's death. We might note that Duckworth and Morgan both promise in their works a recovery of *historical* understanding of Austen. I offer such contortions as presumptive evidence of a certain critical discomfort with *Sense and Sensibility*, both as a novel and as a starting-point for studying its author.

Aside from offering compensatory partisan support for this black sheep of Austen's fictional family, my reading will argue that the work crystallises essential social and aesthetic issues in its author's canon. It acknowledges that *Sense and Sensibility* has had a mixed critical press because its splittings and doublings in the characters of its heroes and heroines, qualities of mind, legal institutions, family structures and class and economic strata have sometimes seemed overly schematic. But it will also argue that the schematism of the work usefully lays bare the audacity of Austen's fictional project, which her growing mastery of her form in *Pride and Prejudice*, *Mansfield Park* and *Emma* tends to mask. A rigorous reading of *Sense and Sensibility* will open surprising vistas on the later and more familiar works.

To the degree that my reading has a thesis, it is both uncomplicated and capacious, and it is not dominated by any particular critical mode or ideology, although its leftward tilt to new historicist and feminist understandings should be readily apparent. To become the first great woman writer in the language, and to devote her writings as she did to the representation of female character, Jane Austen had to remake the novel. Although she had the able examples of such women precursors as Fanny Burney and Maria Edgeworth, Austen never envisioned herself in a gendered ghetto. Virginia Woolf observed shrewdly that even in Austen's juvenile parodies, she was writing for the ages. Her early work, culminating with the publication of *Sense and Sensibility* in 1811, began a process – which ended only with her death – of questioning the adequacy of traditional narrative forms to human experience.

I

Contexts

Historical and Cultural Context

The lexicon through which literary historians describe the culture in which Jane Austen matured has come to be dominated by two topics, revolution and poetry, neither of which would immediately seem useful in clarifying the historical significance of her art. Nevertheless, a compressed *bricolage* of significant dates of Austen's life, matched with pivotal dates in the worlds of politics and letters, may help to situate the novelist and her creations, even if this results in a lesson (salutary, I would hope) in the difficulties of literary history.

Austen was born in the village of Steventon, Hampshire, on 16 December 1775, the seventh of eight children, to the Rev. George Austen and Cassandra Leigh Austen. The year of Austen's birth had seen the battles of Lexington and Bunker Hill in England's American colonies, and by the time she was seven months old, those colonies had declared their independence. Among her generation of writers and artists, all of whom were more celebrated than she during their lifetimes, Austen was five years younger than William Wordsworth, four years younger than Walter Scott, three years younger than Samuel Taylor Coleridge, a year younger than Robert Southey, the exact contemporary of Charles Lamb and J. M. W. Turner, a year older than John Constable, and three years older than William Hazlitt. Without mystifying the 1770s into a decade which brought forth giants, we may safely observe that Austen and her contemporaries were decisively and permanently to shape modern practice and understanding of fiction, poetry, non-fiction prose, aesthetics, and painting and drawing. Without their work, our own cultural histories are simply unimaginable.

Austen began her brief formal schooling in 1783, the year that saw the independence of the United States confirmed by the Treaty of Paris, and concluded it in 1787. As Park Honan's recent biography finally makes clear, measuring Austen's life in terms of international events is not so bizarre as it might appear. Austen's brother Francis, less than two years older than she, entered the Navy's Royal Academy at Portsmouth at the age of twelve. Frank, who would rise to become Admiral of the Fleet, kept scrupulous records of his training, including 'charts and lists of enemy locales or "Countries" of the recent war' (Honan 2). His visits home would have been filled with conversations about the Navy's failures in the war with the colonies.

Perhaps the major personal conduit between the Austens of Hampshire and the great world was George Austen's older sister Philadelphia, who had in fact lived a life as strange as those accounts Austen was to make fun of in her youthful parodies of exotic tales. The story of Philadelphia may seem in one sense a digression from an account of Austen's life and times; in another sense it is crucial to understanding just how much of the world could be visible from a rectory in Hampshire. A spinster without dowry, Philadelphia had sailed to India in 1752 at the age of twenty-one to find a husband. There she quickly married Tysoe Saul Hancock, a surgeon twenty years her senior. When her husband was appointed surgeon at Fort William, Calcutta, in 1759, the family's intimacy with Warren Hastings, a brilliant administrator with the East India Company, began. Philadelphia was rumoured to have become Hastings's mistress, and he was the godfather – perhaps the father – of her only child, Eliza, who was born in 1761 (Honan 43–4; Tucker 39–40).

The Hancock family returned to England with Hastings in 1765, and Philadelphia and Eliza remained there four years later when the men returned to India: Hancock to attempt vainly to salvage their financial fortunes, Hastings to take another posting with the East India Company as second-in-command at Madras. Three years later Hastings was appointed Governor of Bengal. Hancock died in Calcutta in 1775, and two years later Philadelphia and her daughter moved to the Continent, motivated both by the desire to finish Eliza's education and to reduce their living expenses, and settled in 1779 in Paris. There Eliza, clever, diminutive and flirtatious, moved in a social whirl, writing letters home to her repressed and envious cousin in Kent, Philadelphia (Phila) Walter, which laughingly revealed enough of the excesses of the French aristocracy to justify the fall of a dozen Bastilles. She married at nineteen Jean Gabriel Cappote, Comte de Feuillide, beginning a connection from which Austen's father (one of the trustees of a £10,000 fund provided for Eliza and Philadelphia by Hastings) foretold no good. None came.

Eliza returned to England with her mother to bear a son in 1786, and at that time probably first met young Jane Austen, who became one of her particular favourites. Every visit from Eliza opened tantalising prospects on adult experience to the shy adolescent, and Honan has shown well how pervasively the young *comtesse* haunts Austen's later writing (esp. 42–55). It was Eliza who reported back from London on the celebrated trial of her patron Hastings by the House of Lords, which began in 1788 and dragged on until his acquittal in 1795, no doubt furnishing a steady diet of partisan political discourse for the family table; it was Eliza who could make real and material both the splendour of the court of Louis XVI and the effects of the Revolution, because she was back in Paris between late 1788 and at least late 1789 (Tucker 48). Her husband – hapless, faithless and not long lamented – fell as a tragicomic victim of the Terror. Attempting on behalf of the Marquise de Marboeuf to bribe a member of the Committee on Public Safety, he found himself under arrest. At his trial even his mistress testified against him, and he 'appears to have sworn that he was only a poor, scheming, patriotic valet who had murdered the real Comte de Feuillide' (Honan 97). His testimony proving ineffective (or, perhaps, dreadfully effective), he met the blade on 22 February 1794.

The point of this anecdotal history is to suggest how surprisingly well-placed young Austen was in those formative years between eleven and twenty, both to hear the news of the day and to take a personal, family interest in it. The early stages of the French Revolution elicited English responses ranging from horror to delight, and generated a deluge of distinguished political commentary, including Edmund Burke's *Reflections on the Revolution in France* (1790), Mary Wollstonecraft's *Vindication of the Rights of Men* (1790), Thomas Paine's *The Rights of Man* (1791, 1792), Wollstonecraft's *A Vindication of the Rights of Woman* (1792) and William Godwin's *Political Justice* (1792). The impact of the Revolution passed well beyond the stage of ideological speculation and argument in February 1793 when, following the execution of Louis XVI, England declared war on France.

It was during this period of social, political and finally military turmoil that Austen, like the poets who were her contemporaries, began to write. Her preserved juvenilia may date back as far as 1787, and arguably her first mature fiction is the novel-in-letters *Lady Susan*, probably written in 1793–4. The title character, Lady Susan Vernon, is a reluctantly ageing widow – elegant, eloquent, seductive, cynical, wholly amoral, and cold as ice – who is transparently, horrifyingly, and yet somehow lovingly, based on her cousin Eliza. Ironically, Eliza would become Austen's sister-in-law in 1797, marrying her brother Henry, who is a possible model for the rather unheroic hero who narrowly escaped Lady Susan's clutches in the novel.

The years 1794–5 bring us to the approximate date of Austen's work on 'Elinor and Marianne', which will become *Sense and Sensibility*. As my discussion of critical responses to and theoretical perspectives on the novel will suggest, critics are coming to general agreement that the most productive readings of novels are embedded in a meaningful historical context. With Austen, our problems lie in determining the contexts that give her work meaning. The most aggravating impediment for historical contextualists is how very little we know – compared to our detailed knowledge of the evolution of the works of her contemporaries like Wordsworth and Coleridge – about the development of the Austen canon. The paucity of manuscript evidence for the novels and the spottiness of the surviving correspondence, beginning only in 1796 and apparently self-censored as well as family-censored, plague our efforts. What we think we know is that *Sense and Sensibility* existed as an epistolary novel by 1795 and attained something like its published form in revisions of 1797–8 (Gilson 7; Halperin 83–4; Honan 275). Its clear affinities with Jane West's *A Gossip's Story* (1798), which features a character named Marianne who expresses sentimentally romantic attitudes not unlike those of Marianne Dashwood, may argue for a dating no earlier than this (Butler, *War of Ideas* 98–103). What we really know is that it was published in late 1811, advertised on 30 October in *The Star* and 31 October in *The Morning Chronicle* (Gilson 8), the first of Austen's novels to appear in print.

What then, is its historical context? At the simplest level, is this a work of the mid to late 1790s, a time when the property-less but fairly comfortable Austen family was still ensconced in Steventon Rectory, or is it a work of 1809–10, by which time Chawton Cottage had received the diminished family following unpleasant residences in Bath and Southampton entailed by the declining health, retirement, reduced income and death of Austen's father? Are the names of some of its principal characters borrowed, as biographer Elizabeth Jenkins speculated in 1938, from the March 1810 report in *La Belle Assemblée* of two marriages in Hampshire which included the names Elizabeth Steele and Edmond Ferrers (Jenkins 48)? To shift the frame of reference abruptly, does the novel reflect upon and partake of the social and political spirit of pre-Napoleonic England, which we have just glancingly surveyed, or late Napoleonic England? Honan considers *Sense and*

Sensibility primarily in terms of its immediate pre-publication context, losing in the process what I will be arguing are its deep engagements with social topics of the 1790s (275–91). The novel is probably a heavily revised amalgam of attitudes which emerged and mutated over fifteen years, and there can be no definitive description of its relationship(s) to its historical moment(s).

As current criticism suggests, there are many ways of being 'historical'. Reflecting on what you know seems a better way to start than speculating about what you do not, and there is certainly room for wonder in the fact that *Sense and Sensibility* is Austen's first published novel. When she decided, probably sometime in 1809, to change the terms of her commitment to writing by attempting once more to publish her work, Austen had at her disposal three potential novels. A version of what we now know as *Northanger Abbey* was sold to the London publisher Richard Crosby (who also had a financial interest in Ann Radcliffe) for ten pounds in 1803. The novel, then known as 'Susan', was advertised but never printed, and offered back to the author at cost in 1809. A version of what we now know as *Pride and Prejudice* had been rejected by return post by the distinguished house of Cadell and Davies in 1799. And of course she had a version of *Sense and Sensibility*, begun before either of the other books. Had she determined her choice by canvassing her family and circle of immediate friends, *Pride and Prejudice* would have been her hands-down pick, because, as Halperin notes, they never strongly admired or even frequently mentioned *Sense and Sensibility* (94–5). That there was reason for this will, I hope, become clear. First novels are always of enormous importance to writers, and it should be safe to posit that Jane Austen set to work first preparing *Sense and Sensibility* because it was most important to her. It said or could be shaped to say what she wanted to say, in *this* time, in *this* place.

The significance of Austen's decision has recently been underlined by P. J. M. Scott in *Jane Austen: A reassessment*, which offers one of the most interesting reconsiderations of

Sense and Sensibility. Scott works from a splendid essay by Julia Aiken Hodge on Austen's dealings with her publishers. The first novel, as Hodge points out, was taken by Thomas Egerton of the Military Library, Whitehall, 'not a major publisher' (Hodge 81), on terms which were, potentially at least, disadvantageous to the writer. She published on commission: '. . . she paid the expenses of printing the book and took the receipts, subject to a commission paid to the publisher for his handling of it' (Hodge 81). Because the money Austen was venturing had to amount to little less than a quarter and perhaps more than a third of her household's £460 annual income, the risk was substantial. Scott describes the decision, only slightly melodramatically, as 'a single desperate throw of the dice' (84), but he goes on to argue intelligently that there is 'one sole possible inference from this; and that is that, whether or not she thought it the most likely to succeed, *Sense and Sensibility* was the book which Austen most wished to preserve and disseminate' (Scott 85).

There have been several traditional ways of handling Austen's relation to her age, the most prevalent of which has been pure denial that such a relationship exists. The scarcity of historical reference in her works is often taken to indicate obliviousness to great events, except as they affected her friends and family. Richard Simpson, one of her most admiring and influential nineteenth-century critics, remarked in 1870: 'Of organised society she manifests no idea. She had no interest in the great political and social problems which were being debated with so much blood in her day. The social combinations which taxed the calculating powers of Adam Smith or Jeremy Bentham were beyond her powers' (*CH1* 250).

More recent scholars like Alistair Duckworth and Marilyn Butler have detected a stable pattern of social thought in the novels: the politics of self-interest of that segment of the landed class known in the late eighteenth and early nineteenth centuries as country Tories. The history of Austen's immediate and extended families, their local, regional and national economic and ideological alliances and so forth, are taken both as supervening constraints upon Austen's mind and art and as practical constraints upon the range of understandings which may legitimately be inferred from her published writings. We might typify this as the Eliza Problem in Austen studies. It is no trick to demonstrate that much of what Austen knew of the French Revolution was filtered through her cousin the *comtesse*, herself a most ardent royalist. But it is also clear that while Austen loved and admired her dazzling cousin, she was blind neither to her personal limitations nor to the excesses and self-indulgences of the aristocratic life of Paris she had so vividly represented. Consequently, while parts of Eliza find their way into such feisty and independent heroines as Elizabeth Bennet and Emma Woodhouse, parts also become bases for the characters of Lady Susan, Lucy Steele, Isabella Thorpe and Mary Crawford. Must we feel that Austen necessarily always thought as Eliza did about matters aristocratic and revolutionary?

Revisionary accounts such as those of Claudia Johnson and Margaret Doody, to be discussed later in detail, do not deny the class biases of the Austen clan, but they find in the novels themselves clear resonances with contemporaneous progressive social thought, and they support their positions not through global claims about family political tendency but through closely detailed readings of the works. The reading at the centre of my study aspires to this recent tradition, and it chooses to discuss the politics of Austen's novel locally and intensively as it engages central topics of her culture. William Blake said that to generalise is to be an idiot; to generalise about Austen's thought, to take it as something fixed and static rather than something ambiguous and shifting, may be to fall rather lower on the intellectual scale.

Biographical reflections on *Sense and Sensibility* are unavoidable. The relative poverty to which the female members of Henry Dashwood's family are reduced – £500 per year – is still, as Duckworth has reminded us, £40 more than the provision made for the Austen women after George Austen's death (88). To assume that a poor dependent relative of remarkable analytic intelligence will embrace unreflectively an ideology of landed wealth may be pushing the concept of family solidarity beyond its breaking point. The novel's indisputable deployment of themes associated with Edmund Burke, then, may not necessarily assure its endorsement of Burke's positions.

One odd fact should be kept in mind about literary representation in England in the decades surrounding 1800. Austen lived in an age of repression of freedoms of expression that we now unfortunately take for granted. Writing was seldom free, and the list of writers harassed, imprisoned or exiled in the England of Austen's maturity shows that liberties taken were sometimes dearly purchased. As the struggle with France intensified, indirection was more often the order of the day, and we have only recently realised that the obscurities of William Blake's allegories may be attributed as much to his awareness of the watchful eyes of government censors as to his indubitable (and manifold) idiosyncrasies. Austen's earliest work on *Sense and Sensibility* coincided with the treason trials of John Horne Tooke, Thomas Hardy, John Thelwall and others in 1794, the failure of which led to the two 'Gagging Acts' of 1795, which severely restricted freedoms of speech and assembly (Butler, *Romantics* 43, 49). Topics (and habits) of silence and secrecy, so pervasive in Austen's novel, come easily in an age of counter-revolution.

This is not to suggest anything so ludicrous as that Austen was seditious, or ever thought herself in danger of being found so, but that a double-voicedness endemic to texts of the age affects our understanding of her as well. Uncomfortable social understandings expressed through her works – especially those which might seem inappropriate to her extended family's social position and her own social roles as a daughter, sister, aunt and lady – may be implicit and encoded, as Sandra M. Gilbert and Susan Gubar argue in *The Madwoman in the Attic*, rather than enunciated polemically. Consider Austen's cryptic remark to her sister Cassandra about the eagerness of Mrs Catherine Knight to read her first published novel. (Mrs Knight was the wealthy but somewhat officious and oppressive widow of Thomas Knight. The Knights, who were childless, were the benefactors of Austen's brother Edward. He was adopted as their heir and took the name of Knight upon Mrs Knight's death in 1812.) Austen says of Mrs Knight's keenness to see *Sense and Sensibility*: 'I am very much gratified by Mrs K.s interest in it; & whatever may be the event of it as to my credit with her, sincerely wish her curiosity could be satisfied sooner than is now probable. I think she will like my Elinor, but cannot build on anything else' (*Letters* 273). Mrs Knight seems to have been liberal with her advice on the Austen women's move to a property of Edward's, a cottage in the village of Chawton that had been occupied by his steward, in 1809. Austen remarked wryly to Cassandra at that time: 'I am very much obliged to Mrs. Knight for such a proof of the interest she takes in me – & she may depend upon it, that I *will* marry Mr. Papillon, whatever may be his reluctance or my own. – I owe her much more than such a trifling sacrifice' (*Letters* 236). Many of the economic and marital attitudes of the Dashwood women's well-to-do connections seem clearly drawn from Austen's own experience, and her social criticism is forced to walk a fine line – everywhere except in her few surviving relatively unguarded comments to Cassandra. Austen's habits of disguise in her fiction are much like Elinor's in her conversations. The clash between conservative and progressive interpretations of Austen's works, then, is authorised by the texts themselves. What things mean depend on how you read them. Take the following bit of contemporary doggerel as a useful model for reading Austen:

I love my country – but the king	Above all men his praise I sing
Destruction to his odious reign	That plague of princes, Thomas Paine
The Royal banners are displayed	And may success his standard aid
Defeat and ruin seize the cause	Of France, her liberty and laws.

Read straight across, the quatrains express praise of the king and enmity to Thomas Paine and the Revolution in France. Read vertically they oppose the king and praise the Revolution. Since we will engage repeatedly in this study structural principles of linearity and laterality, and make an early acquaintance with Paine himself, the lines comprise a useful motto.

Critical Reception of the Text

The early reputation of *Sense and Sensibility* is forecast on the title-pages of Austen's novels. When this first book was printed at her risk in three volumes by Thomas Egerton in 1811, it was said only to be 'BY A LADY'. The modest first edition, perhaps 750 or a thousand copies, had sold out by July 1813 (Gilson 9), and a second edition was advertised in October 1813 (Gilson 16). Its title-page attests that it is 'BY THE AUTHOR OF "PRIDE AND PREJUDICE"', her second novel, which had been issued in January of that year (Gilson 24). By the time the second edition of *Sense and Sensibility* was published, a second edition of *Pride and Prejudice* had already been released (Gilson 36). This is not to suggest that Austen's first novel was wholly eclipsed or forgotten, because both editions of *Pride and Prejudice* had duly announced their shared authorship with *Sense and Sensibility*. In the absence of an authorial presence as merchandisable as those which caused thousands to await the latest efforts of Walter Scott or Lord Byron, Egerton had to rely on the crudest kind of intertextual reference to build his audience.

When the first edition of *Mansfield Park* appeared in May 1814, the last of Austen's novels to be entrusted to Egerton, its title-page followed his previous practice: 'BY THE AUTHOR OF "SENSE AND SENSIBILITY" AND "PRIDE AND PREJUDICE"'. But when the time came for a second edition of *Mansfield Park*, at which point Austen was shifting to John Murray for *Emma* (1816), rights to *Mansfield Park* were transferred to Murray also, and his 1816 edition claimed only that it was 'BY THE AUTHOR OF "PRIDE AND PREJUDICE"'. The title-page of the first edition of *Emma* also refers only to *Pride and Prejudice*. Finally, on the title-page of the posthumous edition of *Northanger Abbey* and *Persuasion* (1818), the publication of which included Henry Austen's biographical notice of the late author, which constituted the first public announcement of her identity, the works are said to be 'BY THE AUTHOR OF "PRIDE AND PREJUDICE," "MANSFIELD PARK," &c'. While that concluding '&c.' is more than a bit dismissive of *Sense and Sensibility* and *Emma*, it is not entirely out of keeping with the histories of those novels' receptions.

American editions are even more to the point: although Matthew Carey of Philadelphia chose *Emma* (1816) as the only novel to print during Austen's lifetime, its title-page indicated it was by the author of *Pride and Prejudice*; and when he issued all six novels in 1832–3, one was retitled on the spine-label *Elizabeth Bennet, or, Pride and Prejudice*, and all the others had their titles on the spine-labels followed by 'BY MISS AUSTEN, AUTHOR OF "PRIDE AND PREJUDICE"'.

A few salient points can be extracted from this biblio-graphical detail. First, there are decided obstacles to developing an authorial reputation and audience when one declines to be a (named) author. The author of the Waverley novels was able in Austen's day to thrive in anonymity, but primarily by making his namelessness a part of the game with his audience. Despite the numbers of people who knew or learned Jane Austen's identity during her lifetime, her public reputation could only begin after she was dead. As B. C. Southam has shown in painstaking detail, succeeding stages of Austen's growth in public recognition and esteem have usually been set in motion by new biographical revelations for a personality-hungry readership: Henry Austen's brief notice gave her at least a name and station; the publication of James Edward Austen-Leigh's *Memoir of Jane Austen* in 1870 'provided human interest and material for a flood of appreciative essays and reviews' (*Critical Heritage* 2:2); Lord Braborne's two-volume selection of letters in 1884 provided additional grist for the periodical mills; and R. W. Chapman's great editions of the novels (1923), manuscripts (1925–7) and letters (1932) similarly set the stage for major reassessments. Second, while publishers are to their consternation not always able to guess what the public will buy, they are seldom wrong about what it has bought and what it talks about. John Murray, described by Austen as 'a rogue, of course, but a civil one' (Hodge 82), knew in general how to sell books, despite his lacklustre success in promoting Austen. His decision to list *Pride and Prejudice*, in which he had no financial interest, alongside *Mansfield Park* on the title-page of Austen's posthumous volumes (omitting *Emma*, which he had published most recently) is striking evidence that he thought those two works shared her audience's devotion during her lifetime. They were to do so unevenly throughout much of the nineteenth century, as the earlier novel drew to itself those readers who preferred a delightful comic satirist and the latter a smaller and considerably soberer number who fancied a firm but not overbearing Christian moralist. Finally, we might observe, the initial claim on the title-page of *Sense and Sensibility*, that it was 'BY A LADY', itself became contested ground.

We must not make the disregard of *Sense and Sensibility* seem greater than it was. As we assemble the data from Gilson's bibliography, it appears to have been the second most frequently reprinted of Austen's novels in England and America through 1900. *Pride and Prejudice* went through about a third again as many editions, and *Sense and Sensibility* ran close to a dead heat with *Mansfield Park*. *Emma* and *Northanger Abbey* were nearly even, with a third fewer reprintings than those two, with *Persuasion* trailing decisively. The difference in *Sense and Sensibility*'s reputation is revealed by how seldom it was chosen to illustrate those qualities which constitute Austen's greatness. My subject in the remainder of this chapter will be the establishment of Austen's reputation as a major writer and the role of her first novel within that reputation, which was largely the work of her nineteenth-century readers. Her reputation in our own century, which has largely been concerned with understanding the relationship of her work to the history of society and the history of literature, falls more properly under the headings of theory and method, and will be taken up in the chapter which follows.

Walter Scott's 1816 review of *Emma* in the *Quarterly Review* initiated serious consideration of Austen's works. While it speaks briefly but admiringly of *Sense and Sensibility*, it naturally concentrates on the novel under scrutiny. Scott praises Austen's 'peculiar powers of humour and knowledge of human life', admires her disdain for the marvellous and improbable, and gives a solid writerly commendation of her skill in portraiture of characters, which reminds him 'something of the merits of the Flemish school of painting. The subjects are not often elegant, and certainly never grand; but they are finished up to nature, and with a precision that delights the reader' (*CH1* 67). Four years after Austen's death Richard Whately took up Scott's argument in the same magazine, enlarging upon the definition of modern fiction as an art of the probable. Whately praised both the Christian moral soundness of Austen's fiction and the unobtrusiveness of her didacticism: 'She might defy the most fastidious critic to call any of her novels . . . a "dramatic sermon" ' (*CH1* 95). Despite his essay's ostensible occasion, a belated review of *Northanger Abbey* and *Persuasion*, its most compelling remarks are on *Mansfield Park*, while *Sense and Sensibility* goes unmentioned.

In general the nineteenth century read *Mansfield Park* for moral edification, *Pride and Prejudice* for irony, humour and fools (especially the Rev. Mr Collins), and *Emma* – fit audience though few – for the subtle precision of the novelist's art. These, for example, are the novels selected by G. H. Lewes for his praise of Austen's creation of character: 'What incomparable noodles she exhibits for our astonishment and laughter! What silly, good-natured women! What softly-selfish men! What lively-amiable, honest men and women, whom one would rejoice to have known!' (*CH1* 157). Because *Sense and Sensibility* is not well calculated to satisfy moralists, humourists or lovers of 'character', the comments most relevant to it often come either from Austen's detractors or from admiring critics uncertain about the validity of the received portrait of the artist. Margaret Oliphant, one of her most observant admirers, published in 1870 a tribute which was frank about Austen's dark side, which she called a 'fine vein of feminine cynicism' (*CH1* 216). In Austen's first novel, Mrs Oliphant argues, little is really entertaining:

> The Miss Steeles are simply vulgar and disagreeable, and we can scarcely be grateful for the vivid drawing of two persons whom we should be sorry ever to see again. . . . No doubt the foolishness of Sir John Middleton . . . and his wife . . . and Mrs. Palmer . . . are amusing enough in their way; but Marianne's sensibility is not amusing, and we find it utterly impossible to take any interest in her selfish and high-flown wretchedness. Elinor's sense and self-restraint, though so much superior in a moral point of view, are scarcely more enlivening; and the heroes are about as weak specimens of the genus hero as one could desire to see. (*CH1* 222)

Oliphant's criticisms are as perceptive as any early comments preserved on *Sense and Sensibility*, but her overarching vision of Austen as an aloof, uncommitted, critical, cynical female intelligence gives her no way to approach the novel.

The question of vulgarity is most interesting, as it is a persistent refrain of Austen's detractors: Madame de Staël found *Pride and Prejudice* 'vulgaire' (*CH1* 116); John Henry Newman found Austen's clergymen 'vile', and observed that she 'has not a dream of the high Catholic ethos' (117); Charlotte Brontë, who found George Sand 'sagacious and profound', declared Austen 'only shrewd and observant' (126); Ralph Waldo Emerson wrote in his journal in 1861 that Austen's novels are 'vulgar in tone, sterile in artistic invention, imprisoned in the wretched conventions of English society, without genius, wit, or knowledge of the world. Never was life so pinched and narrow' (28). Although *Sense and Sensibility* is seldom mentioned directly in these depreciations on behalf of a fiction which would demonstrate broader moral scope, greater passionate intensity and a more elevated religious sensibility, it more than any other of the novels fits the charges. Its concern with the economics of physical existence is unremitting; its concluding marriage of Marianne to Colonel Brandon has outraged devotees of both pure and fleshly romance; and its fools are more grating, less diverting and more harmful than those of the other novels – Mrs Norris of *Mansfield Park* always excepted.

The stock of *Pride and Prejudice* has remained vigorous until the present day; *Emma* rivals or exceeds it in current reputation; and both *Mansfield Park* and *Persuasion* have attracted the attention and endorsement of major scholars and critics. But until very recently *Sense and Sensibility* has languished in critical reputation, lumped with *Northanger Abbey* as an immature effort – surely an unlikely concept for a work which came from the hand of a writer in her middle thirties who had been at work on fiction for over twenty years – but less charming, less delightful than even that spoof of gothic conventions. What *Sense and Sensibility* has needed is a critical method which can find it interesting both in itself and in its relation to Austen's other works, and especially a method which can envision a purpose for her novels beyond delighting and instructing – those constant staples of earlier critical theory. The key surely lies in refining and extending the notion of Austen's critical intelligence enunciated so clearly by Richard Simpson in 1870.

To comprehend the power of her first novel, one must posit not just an Austen whose analytic powers offer wry reflections on isolated social practices and catch the foibles of individuals, but one who also possesses what Simpson denied her – a commanding and relentless systematic intelligence which rises in her first novel to the level of structural social critique. To the extent that we persist in codifying Jane Austen as the author of *Pride and Prejudice*, we disable our perception of her first novel. Authors change as their historical circumstances change, and successful publication alters those circumstances decisively. *Sense and Sensibility* might best be understood within the Austen canon as an enabling text, which through its financial and critical success permitted Austen's further evolution as a writer, some part of which resulted in her attenuating and redirecting her social criticism. There is nothing mysterious about such a process: as the successful author of a first novel, Austen became a person of enhanced cultural, social and economic standing, more at home in the society her works represent. But we cannot read the unsettling harshness, the palpable difference, of that first novel through our common understanding of the writer it helped her to become.

Theoretical Perspectives

T. S. Eliot remarked somewhere that poems provide ideas so that readers will have something to entertain them while poets go about their business of conducting experiments in prosody. Something of the same could be said about the titles of half of Austen's novels: *Sense and Sensibility*, *Pride and Prejudice* and *Persuasion* all suggest a woodenly didactic, allegorical fictive method in which characters representing one habit of mind do battle with characters representing others. A large body of critical commentary has attempted to formulate the proper proportions of sense to sensibility, wondered whether Darcy represents pride or prejudice or both, and pondered whether and when it is right to bend to persuasion. The best one can finally say of the title of Austen's first novel is that it gave early reviewers something to write about.

When we can learn in Volume I alone that Mrs Dashwood has a keen *sense* of honour, that Margaret has Marianne's romance without much of her *sense*, that Marianne believes with Elinor in Edward's goodness and *sense*, that Marianne thinks a young man in pursuit of pleasure should have no *sense* of fatigue, that Lady Middleton's calmness of manner has nothing to do with *sense*, that Edward thinks his shyness the result of a *sense* of inferiority, that Mr Palmer has an air of more fashion and *sense* than his wife, and that Elinor gives the Steele sisters credit for some kind of *sense* for their cultivation of Lady Middleton through her children, it becomes fairly clear that one word is being asked to do so many jobs that it has ceased to be a very good discriminatory instrument. As critics discover that they cannot say much that interests them about such abstract mental qualities, they unfortunately and prematurely conclude that the novel itself is not very interesting. For those still concerned with the question, Joseph Wiesenfarth answered it more than adequately in *The Errand of Form* (1967): the apparent divisiveness of the 'and' of the title, pitting such qualities as reserve, caution, prudence and calculation against such qualities as feeling, passion, sincerity and outspokenness, turns out ultimately to be genuinely conjunctive, offering a vision of life in which emotion and reflection are mutually supportive (30–59).

Sense and Sensibility is a novel that has remained in waiting for critics to find something in it which interests them and, in turn, a theoretical paradigm capable of articulating their interests. In this century those things have turned out to be, in near serial progression, the novel's passion, its ethics, and its social vision. Recognition of passion arrived earliest. The first genuinely loving commentary came in 1919 from a surprising source, an Irishman and Francophile, aesthete and modernist, the novelist George Moore. 'Remember', he says, centring on Marianne,

> the theme of the book is a disappointment in love, and never was one better written, more poignant, more dramatic. We all know how terrible these disappointments are, and how they crush and break up life, for the moment reducing it to dust; the sufferer neither sees nor hears, but walks like a somnambulist through an empty world. (*CH2* 275–6)

Moore isolates one scene in London to make an overpowering claim for the novel:

> A young girl of twenty, jilted, comes up to London . . . and she sees her lover at an assembly; he comes forward and addresses a few words more to her sister than to herself within hearing of a dozen people, and it is here that we find the burning human heart in English prose for the first, and, alas, for the last time. (276)

Moore rests content in this revelation of intensity, without going on to consider Austen's handling of Marianne's subsequent fate. Other readers who have been captivated by

Marianne's passion have been outraged by her ultimate marriage to Colonel Brandon. According to Marvin Mudrick in *Jane Austen: Irony as defense and discovery*, Austen is frightened by her creation of Marianne, who 'must be humiliated and destroyed. Irony and social convention turn out to be Jane Austen's defenses, not only against the world, but against herself, the heart of passion' (91). Of the novel's ending Mudrick says, 'We may be assured that everyone turns out to be prudently happy, with even a share of domestic satisfaction left for the villain. But we are not to be reconciled. Marianne, the life and center of the novel, has been betrayed, and not by Willoughby' (93). Tony Tanner's introduction to the Penguin *Sense and Sensibility* (1969), later incorporated into his *Jane Austen* (1986), follows largely the line established by Mudrick. (Tanner's work is engaged more directly in the reading which follows.)

The idea of Marianne as a betrayed victim of social convention has migrated to some feminist commentary on the novel as well. In *The Madwoman in the Attic* (1979), Sandra M. Gilbert and Susan Gubar find the novel 'especially painful . . . because Austen herself seems caught between her attraction to Marianne's sincerity and spontaneity, while at the same time identifying with the civil falsehoods and the reserved, polite silences of Elinor, whose art is fittingly portrayed as the painting of screens' (157). In *Jane Austen, Feminism and Fiction* (1983), Margaret Kirkham also regards Marianne's marriage to Colonel Brandon as 'a betrayal of the developed character she has become' (87). The road of passion leads to contrarian readings of the novel, which find their strength in Austen's lack of conscious control of her material. They have the great virtue, absent throughout most of the criticism of the preceding century, of confronting directly the novel's darkness and bleakness. P. J. M. Scott's chapter on the novel in *Jane Austen: A reassessment* builds upon this tradition. For Scott, the novel is two books in one: the first ends comedically, while the second is deeply tragic in its 'powerful portrayal of society's frustrating character', suggesting 'how rarely real fulfillment is realized in the lives of the intelligently, appreciatively deserving' (121).

One final turn of the passionate tradition is represented in Eve Kosofsky Sedgwick's provocative essay, 'Jane Austen and the masturbating girl' (1991). Sedgwick's title – which made her essay controversial in the public press before it was even read at a recent meeting of the Modern Language Association of America – conceals a fascinating Foucaultian analysis of the construction of sexual identity in *Sense and Sensibility*. Sedgwick draws attention to two features of the narrative: that the major passional relationship in the novel is between two sisters, Marianne and Elinor; and that the symptomatology of Marianne's infatuation with Willoughby and nervous collapse upon its betrayal – abstraction, inattention, sensory impairment, restlessness, compulsive movement – bears remarkable affinities to behaviours which will be inscribed later in the nineteenth century in (avowedly) scientific narrations describing the effects of compulsive onanism in young women. Sedgwick likens the punitive pedagogical critique offered by most Austen critics – even by Marianne's defenders and admirers – to the disciplinary cruelty, amounting to clinical torture, sanctioned in one problematic anti-onanist document.

Sedgwick's reaction against ethical criticism of *Sense and Sensibility* is doubly reflexive, because that recent tradition in part formed itself against earlier psycho-social criticism described above. While ethical criticism returns Austen's fable to her own control, accepting Elinor as the rightful heroine of the story, it returns with greater awareness of the ethical problematics of Austen's vision. In *Some Words of Jane Austen* (1973) Stuart M. Tave puts the matter bluntly: '*Sense and Sensibility* is the story of Elinor Dashwood. The action of the novel is hers; it is not Marianne's, and it is not equally divided between the sisters; it is Elinor's. The whole of Marianne's story is included within Elinor's: Marianne's begins later and ends earlier' (96). What critics have failed to see, Tave maintains, is that the novel is less a contest between individualistic strong feelings and socially-sanctioned self-control than an analysis of the proper relationship between language and behaviour. He demonstrates persuasively that the issue is not that Marianne's feelings are particularly strong but that her expression of them is unrestrained. This lack of restraint continually causes pain to herself as well as others. Elinor, on the other hand, carefully guards her language and responds to feeling with action – 'exertion', as the novel has it – which becomes 'the outward and social manifestation of the inward and religious conquest' (113) of self-absorption.

Susan Morgan's *In the Meantime: Character and perception in Jane Austen's fiction* (1980) builds upon Tave's rehabilitation of Elinor in what is perhaps the strongest chapter of a consistently perceptive study. Morgan avoids Tave's pietistic tone, which lends a harsh and unsettling stridency to his depictions of both Marianne and Mrs Dashwood. Instead of seeing Elinor as the proprietress of ethical certainties, Morgan sees her as the one character who has mastered the art of living in uncertainty, the mistress of – though she brings forward Shelley rather than Keats as a model – negative capability. 'For Elinor Dashwood', she argues,

> propriety does not mean giving value to an established set of impersonal social forms. The veil of decorum masks a generosity of heart, an act of love. It is a form of temporising which makes room for our uncertainties and for those sudden moments of understanding which we could wish were more habitual than they are. Politeness is not an adequate expression of our feelings and thoughts. It is really a disguise. And that is its value. It leaves space and time for something still to be known. (131)

While Tave and Morgan provide the closest and most subtly modulated ethical readings of *Sense and Sensibility*, Alistair Duckworth's earlier landmark study, *The Improvement of the Estate* (1971), remains the most influential historical examination of the grounds of Austen's ethics. Duckworth's Austen is a full-fledged disciple of Edmund Burke. Her novels explore exhaustively the idea of the estate, finding in the loss of landed property that faces so many of her characters 'implications beyond the social, implications that are metaphysical or theological in nature' (4). Duckworth's rhetorical strategies in this study are telling: he begins with a close examination of *Mansfield Park* to illustrate, as his chapter subtitle has it, 'Austen's grounds of being' (35–80). Only then does he return to the earlier novels, reading them in the light of its mature social understanding. *Sense and Sensibility* becomes, in his handling, 'an early and rather immature' (ix) work. Duckworth is superb on 'the solidity of financial specification' (86) in the novel, and claims astutely that it is here that 'the vicious cancer of economically motivated conduct is most searchingly analyzed' (88). While he gives due consideration to John Dashwood's callous neglect of his mother and half-sisters, his ethical analysis of the novel falls back upon the contest between the 'private instinct' of Marianne's individualism and Elinor's 'stoical fidelity to traditional and basically Christian values' (111). He never considers that grounding morality on what is at bottom a transfer of wealth and property – the idea of inheritance – may in fact sanction and systematise 'economically motivated conduct'.

Duckworth's study bridges interest in Austen's ethical and social worlds, and now that the word *didactic* can again safely be uttered in mixed company, other historical treatments have built upon his foundation, frequently with far greater attention to other novels of her age. In *Jane Austen and the War of Ideas* (1975) Marilyn Butler places Austen's work among the anti-Jacobin writings of her time, insisting that through a variety of tests – including its distrust of individualism and sensibility, its endorsement of Elinor's 'sceptical or pessimistic view of man's nature', and its advocacy of 'dispassionate assessment of a future husband's qualities' – Austen's first work is an anti-Jacobin novel (194). For all that, Butler concedes, 'we tend to approach Marianne subjectively. She has our sympathy: she, and our responses to her, are outside Jane Austen's control' (196). This rigorous presentation of the most conservative of Austens coincides uneasily with the conflicted and subversive Austen of Mudrick and company. The best parts of Jan Fergus's excellent chapter on *Sense and Sensibility* in *Jane*

Austen and the Didactic Novel (1983) deal less with Austen's relation to fictional tradition than with a detailed examination of the novel's structure, which she reveals to be far more sophisticated than most socially-oriented critics have allowed. She comments that critics who approach the work 'through its connections to the characters, motifs or debates commonly found in eighteenth-century novels' are especially tempted to overlook its achievement, 'probably because their work has entailed reading so many lifeless and mechanical eighteenth-century novels constructed upon similar principles of contrast' (42).

Fergus's conjecture has recently been belied by two brilliantly innovative historical reconstructions of *Sense and Sensibility*, the chapter in Claudia L. Johnson's *Jane Austen: Women, politics, and the novel* (1988) and Margaret Doody's introduction to the Oxford World's Classics edition of the novel (1990). For both Johnson and Doody, Austen's work exists in a far more self-conscious historical and political context than has previously been realised. Along with Alison G. Sulloway's *Jane Austen and the Province of Womanhood* (1989), their work advocates the importance for Austen of progressive writings on the education, social station and political status of women, including the work of radical polemicists of the 1790s like Mary Wollstonecraft. Their analyses share something of the spirit of Mary Evans's *Jane Austen and the State* (1987), a brief overview which argues that Austen offers a radical moral critique of 'the social relationships of bourgeois society' (17). Johnson's and Doody's Austen is a writer of intellectual breadth and coherence, whose work is a participant in urgent human debates rather than a by-product of them. Their versions of *Sense and Sensibility* become, consequently, a novel far more rewarding than any we have previously been given. Although my own approach to the novel was largely formed before their work came to my attention, it gratefully incorporates and occasionally extends their arguments: sometimes, no doubt, to the point where they will find themselves in uneasy agreement at best.

Two more recent theoretical works addressing Austen in some detail deserve mention, even though (or perhaps because) the earlier of the two avoids any mention of *Sense and Sensibility*: Nancy Armstrong's *Desire and Domestic Fiction: A political history of the novel* (1987). Armstrong's work builds from Michel Foucault's studies on the historical construction of sexuality. Her goal is 'to show how the discourse of sexuality is implicated in shaping the novel, and to show as well how domestic fiction helped to produce a subject who understood herself in the psychological terms that had shaped fiction'. She regards fiction, then, 'both as the document and as the agency of cultural history', believing that 'it helped to formulate the ordered space we now recognize as the household, made that space totally functional, and used it as the context for representing normal behavior' (23–4). In practice Armstrong is less interested in those elements of Austen's work which may obliquely reflect late eighteenth- and early nineteenth-century social and political issues and more interested in those through which she creates a language 'that constituted the nuances of emotion and the ethical refinements that seemed to arise from within to modify the political meaning of signs, a new language of kinship relations' (160). From this perspective, the works of greatest interest to her are *Pride and Prejudice* and *Emma*.

Between Self and World: The novels of Jane Austen (1988), by James Thompson, is grounded in the work of Georg Lukács and Frederic Jameson. Thompson is as concerned as Armstrong with Austen's language of feeling, but he is far more interested in the relation of her fiction to changing social practices of her age and makes good use of recent work on British social history. Although Thompson's intent is to historicise Austen's novels, his comparative procedure – with chapters on such topics as clothing, proposals of marriage, the inadequacy of language, representation of character and intimacy – tends to efface historical differences in the development of the canon itself. His most extended discussion of *Sense and Sensibility* occurs in a fine chapter entitled 'Courtship, marriage, and work'.

I have regretfully overlooked here that large proportion of the body of criticism of Austen's work which has been formalistic in character: interested in stylistics, semantics, point of view, dialogue, and so forth. *Sense and Sensibility* has generally not played a leading role in these studies, a number of which are listed with comment in the bibliography. Such studies tend to find their richest rewards in the formal masteries of *Pride and Prejudice* and *Emma*. One observation on this phenomenon could be applied generally to the novel as a form: some overall grasp of the importance of an individual work – call it a critical vision of the novel's fictive vision – seems necessary to energise studies of technique. The final two sections of my reading, dealing with movement and temporality in the novel, are efforts to extend a social reading to matters of aesthetic form.

If my brief overview of tendencies in the critical literature on *Sense and Sensibility* suggests a surprising theoretical consensus underlying disagreements about Austen and her craft, that is neither unexpected nor necessarily to be regretted. Austen's work has come to be definitive of the genre of the novel in that it deals with characters of the middle class, neither greatly superior nor inferior to its implied readers, beset by the commonplace problems of individuals conducting lives impinged upon by economic and social forces largely beyond their control. Scott and Whately saw the normative power of Austen's example so clearly that subsequent critics have been able only to underline that discovery. What Austen's fiction represents is so far beyond dispute that it sometimes appears that strict definitions of the novel are based on her work only, with such adjectival variants as the historical novel, social novel and psychological novel serving mainly to mark deviations from her practices. Our critical differences arise in judgments of how Austen's fiction represents the things it represents, how it depicts and valorises individual desire in its confrontation with social constraint and, especially, as we have seen, how it figures, questions, and values the authority of transpersonal social standards. Astute readers of *Sense and*

Sensibility will not have to subvert misleading oppositions between cultural and natural behaviours, or demonstrate that desire itself is as much a cultural construction as those forces which seek its repression, because the critical intelligence behind the novel has performed these deconstructive tasks for us.

For *Sense and Sensibility* everything in human experience is cultured: Marianne Dashwood's infatuation with Willoughby is as culturally determined as her taste in books and picturesque landscapes; her feelings of joy and pain are genuine, but they are not uniquely individual, as she learns when her sister Elinor shares her own feelings of hopeless love for Edward Ferrars. To say that human experience is culturally coded, though, is not even to begin the work of reading the novel, of teasing out its deployment of those codes and assessing their impact within and upon its characters. One effort at that kind of reading-work lies ahead in this study.

II

Sense and Sensibility
A Reading of the Text

1

Why a Reading?

In *Northanger Abbey*, a version of which Jane Austen had prepared for publication several years before she completed her final revision of *Sense and Sensibility*, our young heroine-in-training Catherine Morland asserted that 'to *torment* and to *instruct* might sometimes be used as synonimous words' (5:110). Catherine had in mind the effects wrought upon unoffending children by the ponderous labours of historians – those who write 'real solemn history' about the 'quarrels of popes and kings, with wars or pestilences, in every page; the men all so good for nothing, and hardly any women at all' (5:108). If Catherine were to attend a scholarly meeting in Britain or the United States today, she might feel that the palms for 'torment' have passed from 'real solemn history' to real solemn literary commentary, although it might be questioned which is being tormented more thoroughly, the listener or the literary text under examination.

At any rate, Catherine (and Jane Austen herself, for that matter) might well want to know just what a critical reading is, and what purpose it is intended to serve. Thirty years ago, at the height of the reign of 'new' criticism, the question would have been easier to answer. A reading would have had as its purpose calling attention to the formal perfections of a work, under the Coleridgean assumption that the establishment of unity in multeity was the ultimate task, and test, of literature. Literature was then widely believed to be – and still is by some – a self-enclosed artefact, answerable only to itself.

Although Austen was served well by this kind of reading – perhaps as well as any novelist before the advent of modernism – *Sense and Sensibility* was not. It has ordinarily been seen as a problem novel, plagued by too many heroines, inadequate heroes, cumbersome plotting, uneven tone, and a most unsatisfactory ending. Those readings which have pulled it into some asserted unity have managed the feat only by ignoring recalcitrant materials within the text. The book has grown in critical esteem only as we have moved past the bugbear of unity to think more seriously about the materials – human, linguistic, social, historical and ideological – that works of fiction deploy. In the process our readings have become more problematic, more troubled, and more willing to face the difficulties of fictional representation.

The reading before you is staged as a series of interventions in the text of *Sense and Sensibility*, intended to locate significant topics of the novel and its craft, to track them as they recur and are revised through the text, and often to measure them against other texts of Austen's age, some fictive, some representing what Catherine would call 'real solemn history'. I will be attempting not to emulate an initial reading of the novel, during which we necessarily hasten to put things together, but a rereading, a slower reading, which has the leisure to observe how things are put together, how they fit, and how they do not quite fit, what problems are resolved, and at what cost, and what problems are never fully resolved. Each section which follows ranges freely through the novel, picking at its threads, occasionally magnifying the text's own disruptions, sometimes clarifying, perhaps sometimes muddling, but always with the goal of empowering alternative readings rather than substituting for them. The ordering of the parts is generally from smaller to larger, from specific to more general topics, and from questions about the novel's represented reality to its means of representation.

2

Wills

Sense and Sensibility is a darker, more serious and more troubled novel than Austen's other two mature works begun in the 1790s. But its peculiar kind of darkness, so often given a psychological reading, is starkly social in nature. Take its opening movement, as stunning a public advent of a new writer as we have ever witnessed. The first two chapters of *Sense and Sensibility* are in the purest sense expository. They introduce the family on which the novel will centre, provide brief descriptions of central characters, create a physical and socio-economic setting, and in general give the necessary background for the action to come, which might be said, since the novel bases its plot on the physical movement of characters, to begin with the removal of the surviving family of Henry Dashwood from the family seat at Norland Park in Sussex to Barton Cottage in Devonshire. But neither Marianne, Elinor, nor Mrs Dashwood appears in a scene, and none of the young ladies' love interests is mentioned. Marianne and Elinor first appear in a scene, and are first given dialogue, in Chapter III. From all indications provided by its first two chapters, the novel will not be about romantic entanglements but about inheritance. This appearance is not wholly misleading.

The first two chapters of *Sense and Sensibility* are fictively excessive. To the degree that their narrative function is to get two young ladies on the road so that they can get about their educations, nothing like the amount of detail we are given on family history, family finances or inheritance practices is necessary. The excess functions thematically rather than narratively, as it pertains to the social matrix in which the characters find themselves rather than the development of their individual characters. For many readers, who have minimised Austen's social and political vision, the chapters are just intrusive, if maddeningly, brilliantly, so. Both contemporary reviewers recognised their power, and the notice in the *Critical Review* closed by reprinting extensive selections from Chapter II (*CH1* 39; 40).

Austen is precise about the succession of the Norland Park estate. The family of Henry Dashwood – including himself, his second wife and three daughters – has lived with his uncle, the current bachelor owner of Norland, for the ten years following the death of his sister. Since Henry Dashwood is described as both the 'legal inheritor' of Norland and the person to whom his uncle 'intended to bequeath it' (3), we can only conclude that the estate lies within the uncle's unrestricted gift. It is not, in the language of the day, under 'strict settlement' during the uncle's lifetime. Were he to die intestate, by common law it would legally pass to Henry Dashwood without restrictions.

That succession is disrupted by the will of the 'old Gentleman' (4), which entails the estate through three generations: providing life tenancies for Henry Dashwood, then for Henry's son John by his first marriage, with the actual inheritor to be on his father's death John's four-year-old son, 'poor little Harry' (8), as his mother is wont to call him. The value of the estate, we are able to compute later, is about £80,000 (its £4,000 annual income multiplied by twenty). One current estimate would make the inherited fortune approximately 16 million in today's US dollars (Brown 7–8; Gaull 379). 'Not to be unkind, however, and as a mark of his affection for the three girls [who have attended him for ten years], he left them a thousand pounds a-piece' (4). Although the equivalent of two hundred thousand dollars is hardly a small amount, the income it would generate – £50 per year – would not permit any of the girls individually to move easily within the class of the gentry to which they were born: 'borderline gentlemen and their families lived on about £700 to £1,000 a year' (Brown 7). One is tempted in this context to recall the generously sentimental grandfather of Austen's adolescent romp, *Love and Freindship*, who miraculously encounters for the first time four grandchildren in the space of five minutes at a Scottish inn. After describing their places on the family tree, with careful attention to birth order ('Philander the son of my Laurina's 3d Girl the amiable Bertha') he hands each of them a fifty-pound note and takes his leave, saying 'remember I have done the Duty of a Grandfather' (31–2).

It should be noted that estates of the magnitude of Norland Park were seldom conveyed by wills, because the current owner would then remain free until his death to change the terms of the settlement of the estate. Normally estates were conveyed by deed upon such an occasion as the coming of age or the marriage of the heir in tail. At such times the life tenant and heir in tail joined to break the existing settlement and resettle the estate. The heir was normally given his independence through an annuity made at this time – a strong inducement for him to agree to restrict his future absolute hold on the property by joining with his father in the resettlement – and suitable provisions could be made for a jointure for the current life-incumbent's widow and portions for the other surviving children (English and Saville 132–40). The will in *Sense and Sensibility* is entirely of the uncle's devising, and Austen chooses for him the mode of conveyance that leaves the Dashwood women most precariously exposed.

Henry Dashwood survives his uncle by only a year, leaving an estate of ten thousand pounds, 'including the late legacies ... for his widow and daughters' (4). All he can do on his deathbed is call for his son and recommend 'with all the strength and urgency which illness could command, the interest of his mother-in-law and sisters' (5). Though lacking 'the strong feelings of the rest of the family' (5), John Dashwood is still moved by his father's request and promises 'to do everything in his power to make them comfortable' (5). What lies within his 'power' becomes the issue.

From some perspectives that power might seem substantial.

He received half the fortune of his mother, described only as 'large' (3), upon his coming of age. His marriage soon thereafter 'added to his wealth' (3). Austen sets up John's fulfilment of his filial obligation beautifully:

> When he gave his promise to his father, he meditated within himself to increase the fortunes of his sisters by the present of a thousand pounds a-piece. He then really thought himself equal to it. The prospect of four thousand a-year, in addition to his present income, besides the remaining half of his own mother's fortune, warmed his heart and made him feel capable of generosity. – 'Yes, he would give them three thousand pounds: it would be liberal and handsome! It would be enough to make them completely easy. Three thousand pounds! he could spare so considerable a sum with little inconvenience.' – He thought of it all day long, and for many days successively, and he did not repent. (5)

We are led to conceive of his father's eighty thousand pounds as an 'addition' to the son's wealth, by no means the bulk of it. By inference, John Dashwood commands a fortune close to that which we will see later in Darcy of *Pride and Prejudice*, perhaps ten thousand a year from holdings of, say, two hundred thousand pounds. Although our figures do not have to be exact to understand how three thousand might be spared 'with little inconvenience', it requires a bit of a stretch to accept his description of his intention as 'liberal and handsome!' (5). And we can only conclude that Austen's ironic treatment of the wealthy gentry's fantasies about its benevolence is mercilessly broad and direct. John and Fanny Dashwood are near to being fabulously wealthy – only 300 to 400 families in England had incomes of over £10,000 a year (Brown 7) – yet they manage to justify giving the Dashwood women not even a crumb.

John's 'repentance', formulated as a recognition of the stern demands of stewardship which entailment entails, begins in Chapter II under the guidance of his wife Fanny:

> Mrs. John Dashwood did not at all approve of what her husband intended to do for his sisters. To take three thousand pounds from the fortune of their dear little boy, would be impoverishing him to the most dreadful degree. She begged him to think again

on the subject. How could he answer it to himself to rob his child, and his only child too, of so large a sum? And what possible claim could the Miss Dashwoods, who were related to him only by half blood, which she considered as no relationship at all, have on his generosity to so large an amount. It was very well known that no affection was ever supposed to exist between the children of any man by different marriages; and why was he to ruin himself, and their poor little Harry, by giving away all his money to his half sisters? (8)

Robbery, impoverishment, half-blood (the precise relationship, if my genetic understanding is good, of a father to his son). John protests, 'It was my father's last request to me', but steadily, in a sequence of enormous power, his intention is whittled to five hundred pounds apiece, then to a life annuity only for the mother of a hundred pounds a year, then to 'a present of fifty pounds now and then' (11), and finally to occasional 'presents of fish and game' (12). As Fanny verbally impoverishes her husband, herself and poor little Harry, she enriches Mrs Dashwood and her daughters:

'Do but consider, my dear Mr. Dashwood, how excessively comfortable your mother-in-law and her daughters may live on the interest of seven thousand pounds, besides the thousand pounds belonging to each of the girls, which brings them in fifty pounds a-year a-piece, and, of course, they will pay their mother for their board out of it. Altogether, they will have five hundred a-year amongst them, and what on earth can four women want for more than that? – They will live so cheap! Their housekeeping will be nothing at all. They will have no carriage, no horses, and hardly any servants; they will keep no company, and can have no expences of any kind! Only conceive how comfortable they will be! Five hundred a-year! I am sure I cannot imagine how they will spend half of it; and as to your giving them more, it is quite absurd to think of it. They will be much more able to give you something.'

Fanny ends in some resentment of the quality of the china and linen Mrs Dashwood will retain: '. . . the set of breakfast china is twice as handsome as what belongs to this house. A great deal too handsome, in my opinion, for any place *they* can ever afford to live. But, however, so it is. Your father thought only of *them*' (13).

A few observations: by the end of Chapter II Austen has broadened the term *will* from a simple legal document into a weapon of family and class warfare. Notice its thudding repetition as an auxiliary verb in Fanny's diatribe: 'they *will* have . . . they *will* pay . . . they *will* live so cheap . . . they *will* have no carriage . . . they *will* keep no company' (12). Wills become purely wilful, simple, arbitrary exercises of power. As Johnson observes (51–2), that surely is the point of Austen's not having placed Norland Park under a tradition of entail in the male line, consequently turning the principle of entailment itself into what Edmund Burke might call an 'innovation'. Further, the chapter is an exercise in perverse hermeneutics, as John and Fanny struggle to understand what John's father could possibly have meant: 'He did not know what he was talking of, I dare say: ten to one he was light-headed at the time. Had he been in his right senses, he could not have thought of such a thing as begging you to give away half your fortune from your own child' (9). 'I am convinced within myself that your father had no idea of your giving them any money at all' (12).

But aside from a thoroughgoing demonstration that John is not a generous son or brother, and that his wife is worse, what is the point of all this? Even Mary Poovey, who is nothing if not attentive to the cultural constructions of women's narratives, finds in the episode little more than a setting of John's and Fanny's actions against an 'implicit system' of 'undeniably Christian values' (*Proper Lady* 184). I would offer, in agreement with Johnson and Margaret Doody, that the values under examination are considerably more specific and local than such a formulation would suggest.

In an essay isolating the features of the Romantic novel, including the work of Austen, Joseph Kestner insisted some years ago that its 'great symbolic subject in both the matter and the method is the *entail*, a legal conception whose essence is restriction and limitation, and whose decisive element is the restriction of choice' ('Jane Austen' 305). He suggested how focus on the entail enabled such writers as Austen, Maria

Edgeworth, Susan Ferrier, John Galt and Sir Walter Scott to explore their twinned themes of law and education, but he offered no historical explanation for the prevalence of the theme. Situated as we now are, both after pioneering feminist studies of Austen by such critics as Doody, Johnson, Poovey, Sandra M. Gilbert and Susan Gubar, Margaret Kirkham and Alison Sulloway, and after new historicist analyses of other writers and of the period generally, we may be able to fit out the foundations and sketch a structure for Kestner's observation.

As Austen assures us, wills, inheritance and inheritance laws have always been the subject of as much private discontent as joy. The emergence of inheritance as a central subject of public political discourse, however, is most easily traced to Edmund Burke's *Reflections on the Revolution in France* (1790), a work whose widespread influence is at last again being taken for granted. Burke's treatise sold 30,000 copies in its first few years and generated no fewer than seventy printed responses by 1793. One of these, Thomas Paine's *Rights of Man* (1791), was reprinted in massive numbers: its circulation has been estimated as having been up to 1.5 million copies (Chandler 17–18).

Burke's premise is familiar, and it has been used to bolster conservative interpretations of Austen's social thought from Avrom Fleishman's *A Reading of Mansfield Park* (1967) and Alistair M. Duckworth's *The Improvement of the Estate* (1971) through the studies of Marilyn Butler to the present. The government of England must be considered as a family. Englishmen 'claim and assert' their liberties 'as an *entailed inheritance* derived to us from our forefathers, and to be transmitted to our posterity' (45). According to Burke, 'the idea of inheritance furnishes a sure principle of conservation, and a sure principle of transmission; without at all excluding a principle of improvement. Whatever advantages are obtained by a state proceeding on these maxims, are locked fast as in a sort of family settlement; grasped as in a kind of mortmain for ever' (45). 'In this choice of inheritance', he continues, we have given to our frame of polity the image of a relation in blood, binding up the constitution of our country with our dearest domestic ties; adopting our fundamental laws into the bosom of our family affections; keeping inseparable, and cherishing with the warmth of all their combined and mutually reflected charities, our states, our hearths, our sepulchres, and our altars. (46)

Burke places his security in the linear family: 'People will not look forward to posterity, who never look backward to their ancestors' (45). Indeed, the linear family serves as a check upon what we might call the lateral family, metaphorically the society living in a given generation, the shallow and selfish discontents of which can lead to dangerous acts of innovation.

Burke further claims that the principle of inheritance is the nursemaid of public as well as private morality:

The power of perpetuating our property in our families is one of the most valuable and interesting circumstances belonging to it, and that which tends the most to the perpetuation of society itself. It makes our weakness subservient to our virtue; it grafts benevolence even upon avarice. The possessors of family wealth, and of the distinction which attends hereditary possession (as most concerned in it) are the natural securities for this trans-mission. (64)

As an experienced member of Parliament, Burke would have known that his argument was playing fast and loose with history. Between 1500 and 1660 current owners of estates had been relatively free to dispose of their properties as they chose (Stone 166), and eighteenth-century entailments were strengthened by relatively new laws and practices. In effect, the viability of strict settlements depended on their being broken and resettled every generation or two. Much of the business of the parliaments in which Burke sat consisted of considering private acts to change the terms of settlements: an average of twenty to thirty such acts per year were executed throughout the eighteenth and the first half of the nineteenth centuries (English and Saville 80). But the point of Burke's hyperbolic identification of family virtue and civic virtue, with inheritance as its governing trope, is not lost on radical writers of the 1790s.

Mary Wollstonecraft, in *A Vindication of the Rights of Woman* (1792), provides a brief sketch noted by Doody (xv) that foresees the situation of the Dashwood women. She imagines girls who are 'weakly educated' – for Wollstonecraft these would be girls not educated for independence – 'cruelly left by their parents without any provision'. They become dependent, then, 'not only on the reason, but the bounty of their brothers. These brothers are, to view the fairest side of the question, good sort of men, and give as a favour what children of the same parents had an equal right to.' But when the brother marries, she goes on to observe, the following occurs:

> The wife, a cold-hearted, narrow-minded, woman, and this is not an unfair supposition, for the present mode of education does not tend to enlarge the heart any more than the understanding – is jealous of the little kindness which her husband shows to his relations; and her sensibility not rising to humanity, she is displeased at seeing the property of *her* children lavished on an helpless sister. (157)

Austen's language in describing John and Fanny Dashwood echoes Wollstonecraft's, though with an even harder ironic edge:

> He was not an ill-disposed young man, unless to be rather cold hearted, and rather selfish, is to be ill-disposed: but he was, in general, well respected; for he conducted himself with propriety in the discharge of his ordinary duties. Had he married a more amiable woman, he might have been made still more respectable than he was: – he might even have been made amiable himself; for he was very young when he married, and very fond of his wife. But Mrs. John Dashwood was a strong caricature of himself; – more narrow-minded and selfish. (5)

Austen softens the economic situation of the Dashwood women, who have an adequate if less than lavish provision, and she complicates the family situation by making them half-sisters. But she also exonerates the father, who is powerless to change the transmission of the estate, shifting the problem of equity squarely on to the shoulders of the inheriting son and his wife. Whereas Wollstonecraft sees a solution for such situations in improved education for women, which would both enable discarded sisters to become economically independent and enlarge the social vision of selfish and narrow-minded wives, Austen provides the materials for a structural critique of the system of inheritance. In this she is closer to Paine.

The Rights of Man argues that social justice in England is poisoned at its source, Burke's governing idea of family inheritance, as Paine provides a scathing account of 'the law of *primogenitureship*' (320). He says:

> The nature and character of aristocracy shows itself to us in this law. It is a law against every law of nature, and nature itself calls for its destruction. Establish family justice, and aristocracy falls. By the aristocratical law of primogenitureship, in a family of six children, five are exposed. Aristocracy has never more than *one* child. The rest are begotten to be devoured. They are thrown to the cannibal for prey, and the natural parent prepares the unnatural repast.
>
> With what kind of parental reflections can the father or mother contemplate their younger offspring? By nature they are children, and by marriage they are heirs; but by aristocracy they are bastards and orphans. They are flesh and blood of their parents in one line, and nothing akin to them in the other. To restore, then, parents to their children, and children to their parents – relations to each other, and man to society – and to exterminate the monster, aristocracy, root and branch, the French Constitution has destroyed the law of *Primogenitureship*. (320–1)

Paine further argues that

> there is an unusual unfitness in an aristocracy to be legislators for a nation. Their ideas of *distributive justice* are corrupted at the very source. They begin life by trampling on all their younger brothers and sisters, and relations of every kind, and are taught and educated to do so. With what ideas of justice or honor can that man enter a house of legislation, who absorbs in his own person the inheritance of a whole family of children, or doles out to them some pitiful portion with the insolence of a gift? (321)

Like Burke, Paine would probably have known that his depiction of the near-abandonment of younger children had little basis in the facts of estate settlement; he is responding to

Burke's fiction of inter-generational continuity with a counter-fiction of intra-generational savagery.

Such are the broad political implications of the discourse of inheritance in the 1790s, a discourse widely enough understood to have been assumed as a given by writers otherwise as far removed from one another as William Wordsworth (in 'Michael') and Maria Edgeworth (in *Castle Rackrent*), both published in 1800 (see Ruoff, '1800' *passim*). Without attempting to demonstrate the indemonstrable, we may safely assume Austen's awareness of it. Her representation of inheritance in *Sense and Sensibility* more closely reflects its polemical role in the debate over political principles than any concrete observation of actual inheritance practices. A discourse that at both political extremes posits the wholesale convertibility of domestic and civic virtue places the emergence of the domestic novel in England in a rather different light than that in which it used to be routinely depicted. Arguably, family history has become political history.

If we set the first two chapters of *Sense and Sensibility* against appropriate passages from Burke and Paine, it is clear, again as Johnson (53) and Doody (xlii–xlv) observe, that they constitute a powerful critique of Burkean claims. Naked self-interest shines through Fanny's concerns for poor dear Harry and the future, even as she rhetorically effaces all concern for herself or the present. Her whining arguments about the tiresomeness of paying annuities to superannuated servants effectively puncture claims that the privileges of the gentry beget a spirit of benevolence, or even a willingness to meet contractual obligations that have been undertaken as a condition of inheritance. It is revealing that at one point John woundedly remarks of his father's request, 'Perhaps it would have been as well if he had left it wholly to myself. He could hardly suppose I should neglect them' (9) – as he then proceeds to do. It is as though John has internalised Burke's assertion of the natural, hereditarily-generated benevolence of his class, and is resentful of an effort to compel him to perform acts of generosity which should come unbidden, even when they will not. John's and Fanny's actions seem inevitably to confirm Paine's critique of hereditary principle: that it provides a schooling in self-interest which blinds its adherents to notions of distributive justice.

What remains to be determined is whether Austen's opening representation of abusive practices suggests a gentry which must clean up its act – reform itself in genuine alignment with Burkean principles – or a gentry which is so far past amendment as to call for other principles for establishing social justice. By definition, apologists display and account for abuses in systems which are under attack, and reformist and radical critiques often share points of affinity. For this reason novelists give us books, not just scenes. Whatever else, we find no relief in John and Fanny Dashwood, whose every reappearance provides evidence of thoughtless arrogance: fresh instances of lavish expenditures coupled with fresh protestations of impoverishment. Nor are they to be written off as upstarts, newer gentry with no understanding of tradition: the Dashwood family 'had long been settled in Sussex' and had been respectable 'for many generations' (3). John may reach his apex of venality, and simultaneously his strongest advocacy of Burkean principles of stewardship, in his reflections on his wife's brother, Edward Ferrars, another victim of parental will.

Edward, who allows himself to fall in love with Elinor despite his secret engagement to Lucy Steele, is an eldest son. His mother controls him by withholding his independence, as his current portion lies in her gift rather than having (like John Dashwood's) descended upon his coming of age. His family wishes to see him take a profession, but not for any potential service to society. Edward is described in this way:

> His understanding was good, and his education had given it solid improvement. But he was neither fitted by abilities nor disposition to answer the wishes of his mother and sister, who longed to see him distinguished – as – they hardly knew what. They wanted him to make a fine figure in the world in some manner or other. His mother wished to interest him in political

concerns, to get him into parliament, or to see him connected with some of the great men of the day. Mrs. John Dashwood wished it likewise; but in the mean while, till one of these superior blessings could be attained, it would have quieted her ambition to see him driving a barouche. But Edward had no turn for great men or barouches. All his wishes centered in domestic comfort and the quiet of private life. Fortunately he had a younger brother who was more promising. (15–16)

Elinor is forced time and again to account for abrupt changes in Edward's mood and behaviour. In general she attributes his gloomy and withdrawn periods to the 'inevitable necessity of temporising with his mother. The old, well-established grievance of duty against will, parent against child, was the cause of all' (102). Austen splits radically the Burkean formula: instead of the will generating in the privileged property-holder a sense of duty, the will becomes an oppressive force which compels the duty of the subject child. Both Austen's presentation and Elinor's analysis of Edward's situation recall, if indirectly, the observations of Wollstonecraft:

Parental affection is, perhaps, the blindest modification of self-love. . . . Parents often love their children in the most brutal manner, and sacrifice every relative duty to promote their advancement in the world. To promote, such is the perversity of unprincipled prejudices, the future welfare of the very beings whose present existence they imbitter by the most despotic stretch of power. (*Vindication* 150)

Mrs Dashwood echoes Elinor's internal language when she attempts to reassure Edward: 'Your mother will secure to you, in time, that independence you are so anxious for; it is her duty, and it will, it must ere long become her happiness to prevent your whole youth from being wasted in discontent' (103). Mrs Dashwood's words are darkly and ironically prophetic, because Edward's literal independence follows his figurative death.

When Edward's engagement to Lucy Steele becomes known, he is disinherited, 'dismissed for ever from his mother's notice' (268). When his 'more promising' younger brother Robert, given his economic independence in a fit of retributive pique by

Mrs Ferrars, later marries the same objectionable young lady, he too is disowned and dismissed. Austen's description of Mrs Ferrars's situation is delicious:

> Her family of late had been exceedingly fluctuating. For many years of her life she had had two sons; but the crime and annihilation of Edward a few weeks ago, had robbed her of one. The similar annihilation of Robert had left her for a fortnight without any; and now, by the resuscitation of Edward, she had one again.
>
> In spite of his being allowed once more to live, however, he did not feel the continuance of his existence secure, till he had revealed his present engagement [to Elinor]; for the publication of that circumstance, he feared, might give a sudden turn to his constitution, and carry him off as rapidly as before. (373)

The linear family, secured by the firm principle of inheritance, seems a shaky cornerstone for the English nation, and Austen's ironic adaptation of Paine's rhetoric of family savagery has more than comic effects. Mrs Ferrars is given to capital punishment, in both its senses. To literalise Burke's term, her hold on her sons is a mortmain indeed.

3

First and Second Sons

Cultural fixation on priority of male birth is illustrated admirably in a late exchange between Elinor and her brother John, who conduct many of the ideologically charged conversations in the novel. This episode occurs while Edward is still 'dead', disinherited and in disgrace with his mother and family. The revelation of his engagement has disrupted his family's plans for him to marry a woman of fortune he has not apparently even met. John himself had described the prospective arrangement earlier in the novel:

> The lady is the Hon. Miss Morton, only daughter of the late Lord Morton, with thirty thousand pounds. A very desirable connection on both sides, and I have not a doubt of its taking place in time. A thousand a-year is a great deal for a mother to give away, to make over for ever; but Mrs. Ferrars has a noble spirit. (225)

The 'noble' spirit, we might observe, is proposing to buy an aristocratic name at a cut rate, a thousand a year in return for her son's control of a fortune that will generate half again as much income. That Miss Morton's father is safely dead, and her portion secure from the claims of potential male heirs, is not incidental.

Edward's acknowledgment of his prior engagement to Lucy causes the family to reconsider its benevolent intentions for Miss Morton:

> 'We think *now*' – said Mr. Dashwood, after a short pause, 'of *Robert's* marrying Miss Morton.'
>
> Elinor, smiling at the grave and decisive importance of her brother's tone, calmly replied,

'The lady, I suppose, has no choice in the affair.'

'Choice! – how do you mean?' –

'I only mean, that I suppose from your manner of speaking, it must be the same to Miss Morton whether she marry Edward or Robert.'

'Certainly, there can be no difference; for Robert will now to all intents and purposes be considered as the eldest son; – and as to any thing else, they are both very agreeable young men, I do not know that one is superior to the other.' (297–8)

Within the linear family, order of male birth decides issues of eligibility and merit. When Robert becomes the eldest son, Edward's opportunistic fiancée Lucy quickly and smoothly shifts her attention to him and entraps him in the course of a few interviews. *Sense and Sensibility* establishes and exploits a structural divide between first and second sons. When both our heroines, Elinor and Marianne, end up married to the *only* second sons depicted in the novel, we need to consider what this symmetry implies.

In order to attain Elinor, Edward must lose his birthright. He dies as an eldest son, and when he is reborn, it is as a younger son. We should take seriously the figure of rebirth for Edward: when he reappears late in the novel at Barton Cottage he is almost unrecognisable. No longer repressed or furtive, he is, as Austen puts it in one of her least ambiguous uses of the term, 'free' (361). He is possessed of 'such a genuine, flowing, grateful cheerfulness, as his friends had never witnessed in him before' (362). He is free of course of his engagement to Lucy Steele, but free as well of the burden of inheritorship, of docilely awaiting his 'independence'. Now he will never be independent, as the gentry terms its freedom from the need to earn money. And he immediately uses his freedom to encumber himself with obligations of a different and happier sort: 'to what purpose that freedom would be employed was easily pre-determined by all; – for after experiencing the blessings of one imprudent engagement, contracted without his mother's consent, nothing less could be expected of him in the failure of *that*, than the immediate contraction of another'

(361). He now must also take a profession, not for the glory of the family line but for his very existence.

He is offered entry into the unfashionable profession he has always found most appealing through a clerical living extended by Colonel Brandon, who is himself a second son and a professional man, a soldier returned from long residence in India. Brandon's early romantic hopes had been blasted by the forced marriage of his beloved to his vicious older brother, a marriage brought about in order to preserve his father's estate, which was 'much encumbered' (205). Brandon's gift of the living is an act of courtesy and compassion – dare one call it political justice? – offered in the face of what Brandon calls the 'cruelty . . . the impolitic cruelty' (282) of Mrs Ferrars's action. This – the most distinctive act of distributive justice undertaken in the novel – is based solely on voluntary association and fellow-feeling. Colonel Brandon empathises with Edward because of what he imagines to be emotional distress paralleling his own, and he values Edward because he knows him to be a friend of Elinor's. The subsequent elevation of Robert Ferrars to the status of eldest son repairs the damage of something like an unfortunate genetic quirk to establish structural symmetry once more. The Ferrars family, unfortunate to have had as its inheritor a young man of quiet intelligence, discernment and humility, is allowed to establish its future claims in one who is idle, dissipated, vain, expensive, noisy and silly.

Colonel Brandon's gift of the living to his brother-in-law calls forth another commentary from John Dashwood, allowing us to observe the linear family's response to an uncomplicated act of compassion and justice:

> 'Really! – Well, this is very astonishing! – no relationship! – no connection between them! – and now that livings fetch such a price! – what was the value of this?'
> 'About two hundred a-year.'
> 'Very well – and for the next presentation to a living of that value – supposing the late incumbent to have been old and sickly, and likely to vacate it soon – he might have got I dare say

– fourteen hundred pounds. And how came he not to have settled that matter before this person's death? – Now indeed it would be too late to sell it, but a man of Colonel Brandon's sense! – I wonder he should be so improvident in a point of such common, such natural, concern! – Well, I am convinced that there is a vast deal of inconsistency in almost every human character. I suppose, however – on recollection – that the case may probably be *this*. Edward is only to hold the living till the person to whom the Colonel has really sold the presentation, is old enough to take it. – Aye, aye, that is the fact, depend upon it.' (294–5)

Colonel Brandon's action is so inconceivable to John that he cannot accept its factuality, whatever the testimony. Colonel Brandon is guilty of breaching conservative principles because he has both given the living outside his family (or connection) and has failed to realise its economic worth to his estate. John Dashwood remains, as always, a man who knows the price of everything and the value of nothing.

Eldest sons, or inheritors, are not a pretty sight in this novel. We have seen enough of John Dashwood to need no further comment, and Robert Ferrars, who replaces Edward in the family line, has no redeeming virtues. Our other inheritors are two sons-in-law of Mrs Jennings, Sir John Middleton and Mr Palmer, and the dominant male character, John Willoughby. Middleton, the distant kinsman who assists the Dashwood women, is good-hearted but empty-headed. Palmer, as Elinor observes, is more difficult to comprehend:

Elinor was not inclined, after a little observation, to give him credit for being so genuinely and unaffectedly ill-natured or ill-bred as he wished to appear. His temper might perhaps be a little soured by finding, like many others of his sex, that through some unaccountable bias in favour of beauty, he was the husband of a very silly woman, – but she knew that this kind of blunder was too common for any sensible man to be lastingly hurt by it. – It was rather a wish of distinction she believed, which produced his contemptuous treatment of every body, and his general abuse of every thing before him. It was the desire of appearing superior to other people. The motive was too common to be wondered at; but the means, however they might succeed by establishing his superiority in ill-breeding, were not likely to attach any one to him except his wife. (112)

From the perspective offered by this unappetising gallery of inheritors – John Dashwood the miser, Robert Ferrars the fop, John Middleton the bluff rustic huntsman, and Mr Palmer the misanthrope – Willoughby seems the answer to a maiden's (and perhaps Edmund Burke's) prayers.

At the advanced age of seventeen Marianne Dashwood has begun to despair of finding a man who could inspire her love. She is somewhat disappointed in Edward Ferrars, whom she considers a less than prepossessing match for her sister:

> '. . . he is not the kind of young man – there is a something wanting – his figure is not striking; it has none of that grace which I should expect in the man who could seriously attach my sister. His eyes want all that spirit, that fire, which at once announce virtue and intelligence. And besides all this, I am afraid, mama, he has no real taste. Music seems scarcely to attract him, and though he admires Elinor's drawings very much, it is not the admiration of a person who can understand their worth. It is evident, in spite of his frequent attention to her while she draws, that in fact he knows nothing of the matter. He admires as a lover, not as a connoisseur. To satisfy me, those characters must be united. I could not be happy with a man whose taste did not in every point coincide with my own. He must enter into all my feelings; the same books, the same music must charm us both.' (17)

For Marianne, a suitor 'must have all Edward's virtues, and his person and manners must ornament his goodness with every possible charm' (18).

We know where the seventeen-year-old Marianne gets some of her notions. She has clearly absorbed her mother's keen sense of honour and romantic generosity (6). Her love for emotionally charged landscape is out of William Cowper, by theorists of the picturesque. She and Willoughby discuss Sir Walter Scott, and they read *Hamlet* aloud together. Margaret Doody interestingly traces Willoughby's lineage as a romantic hero. Like Valancourt of Ann Radcliffe's *The Mysteries of Udolpho*, he first appears in hunting garb with dogs and a gun:

> Valancourt comes to the rescue of the heroine and her father, if by the commonplace expedient of informing them of their way.

Willoughby is Marianne's 'preserver' – according to Margaret's inaccurate description. Marianne ought, however, to beware. If Willoughby comes upon her like Harriet Byron's 'preserver' Sir Charles Grandison, he is also ... a villainous rake like Sir Hargrave Pollexfen. If he appears as a Valancourt, he has some of the dangerous qualities of a money-loving Montoni – the villain with whom Catherine too literally identified General Tilney [in *Northanger Abbey*]. Willoughby's name echoes that of a character in another novel. In Frances Burney's *Evelina* the heroine is accosted at her second ball by Sir Clement Willoughby, who 'began a conversation, in that free style which only belongs to old and intimate acquaintance'. Evelina's reduced situation in the world, combined with her refined education, elegant manners, and beauty, would seem to point her out to this Willoughby as ideally qualified to be the mistress of a fashionable man – a danger not remote from one in Marianne Dashwood's situation. (xxvii–xxviii)

Doody's suggestions could be pushed further: Valancourt remains the hero of *Udolpho*, but not without incurring the reader's impatience with his self-dramatising and absurdly self-pitying character, and not without having his reputation tainted by exaggerated charges of dissipations – gambling and debauchery – similar to those proved against Willoughby; and Austen's Willoughby is close to being a perfected version of Burney's, as we shall see below. However, Marianne's ideas about perfect suitors do not appear to be literarily induced. Unlike Catherine Morland of *Northanger Abbey*, one or more versions of which Austen had completed before publishing *Sense and Sensibility*, Marianne is not presented as a reader of novels or romances, gothic or otherwise.

That her receptivity to Willoughby is none the less culturally coded seems apparent, however, and the mention of Scott provides one clue. Willoughby enters the scene as a chivalric figure assisting a maiden in distress. Running exuberantly down a hill to escape a sudden shower, Marianne twists her ankle and cannot walk. Willoughby appears, a 'gentleman carrying a gun' (42), and takes immediate control of the situation:

... perceiving that her modesty declined what her situation rendered necessary, [he] took her up in his arms without farther delay, and carried her down the hill. Then passing through the garden, the gate of which had been left open by Margaret, he bore her directly into the house, whither Margaret was just arrived, and quitted not his hold till he had seated her in a chair in the parlour. (42)

Austen's archaisms ('whither', 'quitted not his hold') help to signal Willoughby's lineage.

After Willoughby departs, his 'manly beauty', 'more than common gracefulness' and 'gallantry' dominate the conversation, and Marianne has soon cast him as a character worthy of her love:

His person and air were equal to what her fancy had ever drawn for the hero of a favourite story; and in his carrying her into the house with so little previous formality, there was a rapidity of thought which particularly recommended the action to her. Every circumstance belonging to him was interesting. His name was good, his residence was in their favourite village, and she soon found out that of all manly dresses a shooting-jacket was the most becoming. Her imagination was busy, her reflections were pleasant, and the pain of a sprained ancle was disregarded.

Susan Morgan remarks perceptively that if 'there is a conservative in this novel, a character who stands against adaptation and change, who upholds a fixed version of meaning and value ... that character is Marianne' (*In the Meantime* 119). Marianne's responses to Willoughby look back to preliterate codes, a world of childhood fairy-tales with endangered maidens and handsome princes. They are certainly not the stuff of the novel, that form of bourgeois romance that is most insistent that surface illusions be penetrated. She would be better off if she were an avid reader of Radcliffe, and in an odd way the naive Catherine Morland of *Northanger Abbey* is further along the road to useful literary sophistication than Marianne. We might charitably call Marianne's illusions chivalric nonsense (a phrase Paine uses in characterising Burke's treatise) with too many cultural sources to be traced profitably. Notable absences and presences may be remarked, however: one place these codes will not be found valorised is in the radical literature of the 1790s, and one place they are everywhere is in the writings of Burke.

The seed source of the code of chivalry for late eighteenth- and early nineteenth-century culture may be Burke's description of young Marie Antoinette:

> It is now sixteen or seventeen years since I saw the queen of France, then the dauphiness, at Versailles; and surely never lighted on this orb, which she hardly seemed to touch, a more delightful vision. I saw her just above the horizon, decorating and cheering the elevated sphere she just began to move in, – glittering like the morning-star, full of life, and splendour, and joy. Oh! what a revolution! and what an heart must I have, to contemplate without emotion that elevation and that fall! Little did I dream that. . . I should live to see such disasters fallen upon her in a nation of gallant men, in a nation of honour and of cavaliers. I thought ten thousand swords must have leaped from their scabbards to avenge even a look that threatened her with insult. – But the age of chivalry is gone. – That of sophisters, oeconomists, and calculators, has succeeded; and the glory of Europe is extinguished. Never, never more, shall we behold that generous loyalty to rank and sex, that proud submission, that dignified obedience, that subordination of the heart, which kept alive, even in servitude itself, the spirit of an exalted freedom. The unbought grace of life, the cheap defence of nations, the nurse of manly sentiment and heroic enterprize is gone! It is gone, that sensibility of principle, that chastity of honour, which felt a stain like a wound, which inspired courage while it mitigated ferocity, which ennobled whatever it touched, and under which vice itself lost half its evil, by losing all its grossness. (89)

When Burke recollects his encounters with members of the French nobility, he describes a class

> for the greater part composed of men of a high spirit, and of a delicate sense of honour, both with regard to themselves individually, and with regard to their whole corps, over whom they kept, beyond what is common in other countries, a censorious eye. They were tolerably well-bred; very officious, humane, and hospitable; in their conversation frank and open; with a good military tone; and reasonably tinctured with literature, particularly of the authors in their own language. (151)

If we note Willoughby's critical disdain for the personal failings of others of his class – the shallowness and lack of taste of the Middleton clan and the stuffiness he finds in Colonel Brandon – and allow a manly shooting jacket and spirited riding to the hounds stand in for 'good military tone', we have here a just description of the virtues of Willoughby, or at least the appearance of those virtues. The descriptors that cluster around him – grace, charm, taste, frankness, manliness, honour, spirit – are also the attributes of Burke's chivalric nobility. Indeed, as Carol Kay has observed, Burke is trying in the *Reflections* 'to make England into ancien-régime France, the pattern of the old common and even of the courtly manners that were always associated with France' (*Political Constructions* 276).

Sense and Sensibility goes on to reveal that this young knight has only clothes, only the visible manifestations of virtue and none of the thing itself. Initially poised against John Dashwood, who could be the living incarnation of Burke's degraded company of 'sophisters, oeconomists, and calculators', Willoughby proves ultimately to be just another and more dangerous of them – more dangerous because wholly plausible. Trying to justify his behaviour in his final interview with Elinor, Willoughby declares:

> My fortune was never large, and I had always been expensive, always in the habit of associating with people of better income than myself. Every year since my coming of age, or even before, I believe, had added to my debts; and though the death of my old cousin, Mrs. Smith, was to set me free; yet that event being uncertain, and possibly far distant, it had been for some time my intention to re-establish my circumstances by marrying a woman of fortune. (320)

Willoughby callously glosses over his seducing and discarding Colonel Brandon's ward Eliza, revealing to Elinor a character more depraved than he is able to conceive or willing to admit. Burke may have been willing to overlook 'vice' when it is divested of its 'grossness', but Austen was not. Elinor reflects silently on the irreparable injury which too early an independence and its consequent habits of idleness, dissipation, and luxury, had made in the mind, the character, the happiness of a man who, to every advantage of person and talents, united a disposition open and honest, and a feeling, affectionate temper. The world had made him extravagant and vain – Extravagance and vanity had made him cold-hearted and selfish. (331)

The echo of the opening description of John Dashwood could hardly be clearer: 'He was not an ill-disposed young man, unless to be rather cold hearted, and rather selfish, is to be ill-disposed' (5). The potential saving remnant of the inheritor class – its redeeming first son – provides its final condemnation. The novel will approve a far less spectacular constellation of virtues in its genuine heroes.

While Willoughby has seemed the model of the young chivalric gentleman, it is throughout the novel Colonel Brandon, whose early life had been ruined by patriarchal tyranny, who enacts the virtues of chivalry. Despite his seeking the constitutional safeguard of a flannel vest, it is he who has been a soldier rather than a hunter, who has lived in the exotic East, who has ridden to the rescue of his ward Eliza, who has faithfully worshipped Marianne from afar, who has challenged Willoughby to a duel, and who has assisted the outcast Edward. One of the fine comic moments of the novel comes when Mrs Dashwood, so early and easy a victim of Willoughby's chivalric charm, modifies and reattaches his pretended virtues to Colonel Brandon:

'And his manners, the Colonel's manners are not only more pleasing to me than Willoughby's ever were, but they are of a kind I well know to be more solidly attaching to Marianne. Their gentleness, their genuine attention to other people, and their manly unstudied simplicity is much more accordant with her real disposition, than the liveliness – often artificial, and often ill-timed of the other. I am very sure myself, that had Willoughby turned out as really amiable; as he has proved himself the contrary, Marianne would yet never have been so happy with *him*, as she will be with Colonel Brandon.' (338)

Elinor, to whom these words are addressed, 'could not quite

agree' with them, but she could hardly disagree that so far as chivalric virtues are valuable and have survived, they have not been preserved through the system of primogeniture.

4

First and Second Attachments

One of Marianne's most firmly held opinions, which correlates well with her improbably high standards in a suitor, is her belief in the singularity and immutability of passionate relationships. One can genuinely love but once, and second attachments can only be arrangements for economic security and social convenience. The subject is broached in a conversation between Elinor and Colonel Brandon, who has fallen in love with Marianne and must stand by watching her openly and affectionately return the signs of partiality Willoughby seems to radiate:

> His eyes were fixed on Marianne, and, after a silence of some minutes, he said with a faint smile, 'Your sister, I understand, does not approve of second attachments.'
> 'No,' replied Elinor, 'her opinions are all romantic.'
> 'Or rather, as I believe, she considers them impossible to exist.'
> 'I believe she does. But how she contrives it without reflecting on the character of her own father, who had himself two wives, I know not. A few years however will settle her opinions on the reasonable basis of common sense and observation; and then they may be more easy to define and to justify than they now are, by any body but herself.'
> 'This will probably be the case,' he replied; 'and yet there is something so amiable in the prejudices of a young mind, that one is sorry to see them give way to the reception of more general opinions.' (55–6)

Marianne's belief that one can love but once is accompanied by a corollary that love is the province of the young:

'A woman of seven and twenty,' said Marianne, after pausing a moment, 'can never hope to feel or inspire affection again, and if her home be uncomfortable, or her fortune small, I can suppose that she might bring herself to submit to the offices of a nurse, for the sake of the provision and security of a wife. In his marrying such a woman therefore there would be nothing unsuitable. It would be a compact of convenience, and the world would be satisfied. In my eyes it would be no marriage at all, but that would be nothing. To me it would seem only a commercial exchange, in which each wished to be benefited at the expense of the other.' (38)

The 'amiability' that Colonel Brandon is able to find in Marianne's youthful 'prejudices' (another Burkean code-word) is provided by her societal context. Given the over-whelmingly economic view of marriage in her society, her repudiation of pragmatic justifications for marriage is under-standable. But her recourse, which is to remove personal attraction from the influence of the general web of social concerns, and consequently place it outside the considerations that govern them, seems doomed to failure.

While Marianne may insist that the attraction one young person feels for another is a phenomenon outside the reach of market forces, her brother John effortlessly commoditises physical attractiveness. In a remarkable scene following Marianne's debilitating illness, John confides to Elinor:

'She was as handsome a girl last September, as any I ever saw; and as likely to attract the men. There was something in her style of beauty, to please them particularly. I remember Fanny used to say that she would marry sooner and better than you did; not but what she is exceedingly fond of *you*, but so it happened to strike her. She will be mistaken, however. I question whether Marianne *now*, will marry a man worth more than five or six hundred a-year, at the utmost, and I am very much deceived if *you* do not do better.' (227)

Given the prevalence of such calculations, Marianne adopts a strenuous doctrine of romantic purity, which in effect insists that romantic relationships are unlike all other relationships. If the young feel affection for one another, what those slightly older than them feel cannot be affection at all. A marriage that is based on any consideration other than pure emotion must then be no marriage at all.

It is this conception of love as pure difference that leads Marianne into behaviour toward Willoughby that at best makes her emotions the sport of the small, gossipy community in which she lives and at worst leads her into acts of impropriety, notably her visit with Willoughby to his aunt Mrs Smith's estate while the lady herself is absent. No reader has registered more strongly than Doody the force of Marianne's violation here, not just of a given society's narrow codes of propriety, but rules of genuine civility and taste which, when breached by others, she is the first to deplore (xxx–xxxi). When Marianne is upbraided by Elinor for the visit, her response is to apply a simple emotional test: '. . . if there had been any real impropriety in what I did, I should have been sensible of it at the time, for we always know when we are acting wrong, and with such a conviction I could have had no pleasure' (68). Love is outside the social concerns of life, and the only possible arbiter of behaviour in love is feeling. For all her occasional bridling at social conventions, Marianne is not a natural outlaw. Only in matters of the heart does she allow herself flagrantly to step outside social obligations. The danger of her ideology of romantic love, of course, is precisely its conviction that pleasure is all. It has led her into this ethical trespass; it will lead her to seek Willoughby's attention through clandestine correspondence; and it will lead her into a frantic pursuit of him when she visits London. There is ultimately no place it could not lead her, because it acknowledges no limits.

Marianne's views have this in common with her mother's: they make it extremely difficult for Elinor to discover an emotional lexicon which will allow her to discuss with them her puzzling relationship with Edward. Describing Edward to her mother, Elinor says:

> 'I think you will like him,' said Elinor, 'when you know more of him.'

'Like him!' replied her mother with a smile. 'I can feel no
sentiment of approbation inferior to love.'
   'You may esteem him.'
   'I have never yet known what it was to separate esteem and
love.' (16)

When Elinor talks with Marianne, she encounters even stronger
opposition:

'I do not attempt to deny,' said she, 'that I think very highly of
him – that I greatly esteem, that I like him.'
   Marianne here burst forth with indignation –
   'Esteem him! Like him! Cold-hearted Elinor! Oh! worse than
cold-hearted! Ashamed of being otherwise. Use those words
again and I will leave the room this moment.' (21)

For Marianne romantic feeling exists apart from ordinary and
continuous social feelings. It presents an utter break in one's
existence. While the novel explores the sheer emotional power
of romantic attachment more thoroughly than Austen's other
works – and perhaps more sympathetically – it ultimately finds
it disastrously inadequate.

Austen's writings before the publication of *Sense and
Sensibility* had generally treated idealisations of romantic love
more comically – sometimes hysterically. Her adolescent romp
Love and Freindship sent up nearly every possible variant on
love at first sight, eternal devotion and the devastation wrought
by a broken heart (which is, she tells us, more likely to be fatal
if manifested in fainting spells than in frenzy fits). *Northanger
Abbey* had good clean fun with Catherine Morland's many
shortcomings as a heroine of sensibility, ending in the mortify-
ing truth of the origin of Henry Tilney's love for her:

. . . though Henry was now sincerely attached to her, though he
felt and delighted in all the excellencies of her character and truly
loved her society, I must confess that his affection originated
in nothing better than gratitude, or in other words, that a
persuasion of her partiality for him had been the only cause
of giving her a serious thought. It is a new circumstance in
romance, I acknowledge, and dreadfully derogatory of an
heroine's dignity; but if it be as new in common life, the credit of
a wild imagination will at least be all my own. (5:243)

Perhaps more directly to the point, in *Pride and Prejudice* Elizabeth Bennet's love for Darcy grows from her esteem for his character, discovered belatedly, and her attraction to the superficial charms of Wickham – a sort of degraded and far less plausible stand-in for Willoughby – fades as her understanding of Darcy's human value grows.

The novels yet to be written will even more thoroughly muddle any attempts to separate romantic love from other human attachments. *Mansfield Park* will flirt with incest in giving us a love between Fanny Price and her cousin Edmund Bertram, who has throughout the novel stood in the place of an older brother. *Emma* similarly gives us a tale in which the spirited heroine discovers with a shock of revelation that Mr Knightley, the brother-in-law who has served as her paternal superego – nagging, restraining, shaping and guiding her behaviour – must marry no one other than herself. And finally *Persuasion* tells the story of a first attachment that becomes a second attachment, as Anne Elliot and Captain Wentworth, separated in bitter hopelessness for seven years, rediscover their mutual attraction and esteem.

While Mrs Dashwood may not know how to separate love and esteem, Austen always has, and she knows that esteem may be more productive of love than the reverse. When Darcy solicits Elizabeth's hand in marriage, Mr Bennet's concern is not that she please her heart, but that she please her mind:

> 'I know your disposition, Lizzy, I know that you could be neither happy nor respectable, unless you truly esteemed your husband; unless you looked up to him as a superior. Your lively talents would place you in the greatest danger in an unequal marriage. You could scarcely escape discredit and misery. My child, let me not have the grief of seeing *you* unable to respect your partner in life. You know not what you are about.' (2:376)

Mr Bennet's language is veiled, but his meaning is clear. This appeal comes even after Elizabeth has protested her love for Darcy. The threat he sees for Elizabeth is that marriage without esteem, whether for attraction or riches, would lead her out of respectability, perhaps into the condescending mockery that characterises his own relationship with Mrs Bennet, perhaps even into the moral discredit of illicit liaisons characteristic of women as well as men among the unequally and unhappily married gentry.

Mr Bennet's concerns, like those of *Sense and Sensibility* generally, coincide remarkably with the observations of Wollstonecraft, who surely earned her right to speak of the relative claims of passion and regard, and who was strong on behalf of the educative value of prior attachments:

> Personal attachment is a very happy foundation for friendship; yet, when even two virtuous young people marry, it would be happy if some circumstances checked their passion; if the recollection of some prior attachment, or disappointed affection, made it on one side, at least, rather a match founded on esteem. In that case they would look beyond the present moment, and try to render the whole of life respectable, by forming a plan to regulate a friendship which only death ought to dissolve.
>
> Friendship is a very serious affection; the most sublime of all affections, because it is founded on principle, and cemented by time. The very reverse may be said of love. In a great degree, love and friendship cannot subsist in the same bosom; even when inspired by different objects they weaken or destroy each other, and for the same object can only be felt in succession. The vain fears and fond jealousies, the winds which fan the flame of love, when judiciously or artfully tempered, are both incompatible with the tender confidence and sincere respect of friendship. (167–8)

Although Austen is never so pessimistic as to deny the possible coexistence of love and friendship, the sad fates of marriages founded on the charms of feminine beauty, that polite term for sexual attraction – the Middletons and Palmers in *Sense and Sensibility*, the Bennet parents and Lydia and Wickham in *Pride and Prejudice* – as well as the fortuitously aborted attractions between Marianne and Willoughby, Edward Ferrars and Lucy Steele, and Elizabeth and Wickham, suggest that she would have strongly seconded Wollstonecraft's central teachings.

Marianne will not listen to esteem where she wants to hear of love. The painful course of her attachment to Willoughby, which grows before esteem for anything other than his charm could be rationally possible, and continues well after his behaviour towards her and Colonel Brandon's ward Eliza has rendered esteem impossible, is a stern education in the perils of romance. Just how stern the lesson is may be seen in sharply contrasting responses to the fate of Marianne among highly sophisticated critical readers, as they are usefully signalled in the two major competing classroom editions of the novel.

The passage at issue involves Marianne's virtual recantation of her ideas on first attachments, as claimed by the narrator on the basis of her actions. After Elinor and Edward have settled in the parsonage at Delaford, Mrs Dashwood and her other daughters spend 'much more than half their time' with them. As the novel observes, this is as much policy as affection on Mrs Dashwood's part, as her 'darling object' is to bring Marianne and Colonel Brandon together. Edward and Elinor eagerly join in this 'confederacy against her'. Here is how the novel handles Marianne's apostasy:

> Marianne Dashwood was born to an extraordinary fate. She was born to discover the falsehood of her own opinions, and to counteract, by her conduct, her most favourite maxims. She was born to overcome an affection formed so late in life as at seventeen, and with no sentiment superior to strong esteem and lively friendship, voluntarily to give her hand to another! – and *that* other, a man who had suffered no less than herself under the event of a former attachment, whom, two years before, she had considered too old to be married, – and who still sought the constitutional safeguard of a flannel waistcoat!
>
> But so it was. Instead of falling a sacrifice to an irresistible passion, as once she had fondly flattered herself with expecting, – instead of remaining even for ever with her mother, and finding her only pleasures in retirement and study, as afterwards in her more calm and sober judgment she had determined on, – she found herself at nineteen, submitting to new attachments, entering on new duties, placed in a new home, a wife, the mistress of a family, and the patroness of a village. (378–9)

Tony Tanner admits that there are two ways to respond to this passage:

> One can feel that there is something punitive in the taming of
> Marianne and all she embodies, indeed one might think that
> something is being vengefully stamped out. It is as though Jane
> Austen had gone out of her way to show that romantic feelings
> are utterly non-viable in society. (31)

From this perspective, Marianne can even be felt to have died:
'Whatever the name of the automaton which submits to the
plans of its relations and joins the social game, it is not the real
Marianne, and in the devitalised symmetry of the conclusion
something valuable has been lost' (32). Another reading might
'applaud the hard-headed realism which recognizes that the
consolations of society are only achieved at the cost of a
more or less rigorous curbing of the intensities of impulse
and a disciplined diminishment in the indulgence of solitary
emotional fantasies' (32). But Tanner's sympathies are vividly
registered through his rhetorical force, and he would prefer for
Marianne death before such dishonour. It will remain for
Emily Brontë, he says, to 'show social structure dissolving
before the unanswerable force of individual passion' (33).

Tanner's analysis insists on an absolute division between
nature and nurture without, despite occasional nods to Michel
Foucault, considering the 'natural' as itself a social construct.
In this oversight, his preface seems to be a child of its time,
the late 1960s, when naturalness, passion and individuality
expressed their uniqueness in a surprisingly uniform code of
dress and misbehaviour. Marianne's passionate attachment to
Willoughby is no more natural than her love of Cowper or
Scott or her sense of the picturesque. And it might be wondered whether her notion of intense singular attachment is not
actually in keeping with patriarchal notions of woman's social
function. Doody's corrective analysis sees at least two social
codes enacted in the novel, one by the set of characters who
tie their lives to primacy and primogeniture, another among
that set who create a more humane social structure in their
secondariness:

> The selfish and strong who opt to live on the first (but inferior)
> level of inheritance, power, and control (mixed in with however

much boredom and obsequiousness) are not punished, apart from living as themselves; only Willoughby among this crowd is wise enough to regret this fate to any degree. Others who changed in their love changed for the better. Marianne 'could never love by halves; and her whole heart became, in time, as much devoted to her husband, as it had once been to Willoughby'. . . . Hearts mend; life moves. Flexibility and grace are needed, not hopeless ideal constancy. The knowing sense that sees the inadequacy of human society and the terrible greed evoked by many of its institutions and practices must be tempered by the sensibility that can appreciate the opportunity of loving – even of loving again. (xlvi)

Doody's analysis echoes perfectly the apparent intentions of Austen's text, and it answers well to what most of us know as the reality of human experience. That Tanner's romantic analysis still retains its terrible pull – tempting us to prefer the uncompromised deaths of Catherine Earnshaw and Heathcliff to the continued life and asserted happiness of Marianne – suggests how small a distance we have come toward extricating ourselves from the code of romantic love, with its proclivity for fainting spells and frenzy fits, for vows of eternal devotion fulfilled through violent death. Most importantly, though, Tanner recognises only one 'social game' played out in a monolithic social order. As Doody insists, *Sense and Sensibility* provides the opportunity for its characters to choose and make their societies, and it sketches possibilities that can enhance as well as suppress the individual spirit.

5

Linear and Lateral Families

The opening section of this reading explored the legal construction and propagation of what I have called the linear family, the family as it is defined through the principles and practice of inheritance law. It also suggested the consequences awaiting those who lie outside the line of familial succession by virtue of their 'inferior' sex or birth-order, whether natural or, in the case of Edward Ferrars, self-created. It is time to explore in greater detail the impact of the structural principle of linearity on family behaviours in *Sense and Sensibility* and to explore the social practices that develop among those – by far the majority of the important characters in the novel – whose fate it is to live outside the charmed line of descent.

Although the families of *Sense and Sensibility* are nominally patriarchal in their constitution, their social behaviours are anything but dominated by a male hierarchy. Indeed, by any conventional measures of social power and influence, the two strongest characters in the book are two matriarchs, Mrs Jennings, who has successfully married off two attractive but otherwise worthless daughters, and Mrs Ferrars, who tyrannises her two sons and anyone else who ventures within earshot. It may be most interesting, though, to look at the role played by children, to which Doody has indirectly called attention through her sensitive discussion of mothering in the novel (xxi–xxvii). The work does not dwell on the lives of the heroines as children, a subject whose importance Austen will not fully exploit until *Mansfield Park*, but other people's children.

John and Fanny Dashwood constitute the perfect linear family: John is an only son, Fanny a first wife, and little Harry a first son and only child, so far as the novel goes. We suspect he will remain so, because additional children would surely violate his parents' strict notions of economy, which might be described as accumulating the greatest possible wealth for the smallest possible number of people. It is little Harry who brings about the crucial alteration in the lives of the second Mrs Dashwood and her daughters:

> The whole [of the uncle's fortune] was tied up for the benefit of this child, who, in occasional visits with his father and mother at Norland, had so far gained on the affections of his uncle, by such attractions as are by no means unusual in children of two or three years old; an imperfect articulation, an earnest desire of having his own way, many cunning tricks, and a great deal of noise, as to outweigh all the value of all the attention which, for years, he had received from his niece and her daughters. (4)

And it is young Harry's interest, we remember, to which Fanny Dashwood appeals in guarding against every half-hearted attempt by her husband to think of something convenient to do toward honouring his father's dying wish. She stages her protests as though mothers and children must be constantly in league against the terrors of deprivation and abandonment, despite the obvious fact that the estate of Norland Park has reached John Dashwood at all only so that it may find its way ultimately to poor little Harry. Of course, in a novel in which we are given three widows and no widowers, and in which Mrs Dashwood has been left through his wife's connivance to sink or swim by her only son, Fanny's frenzied bonding with her son and his interests is not without its cultural shrewdness. Fanny is fond of quoting odds ('ten to one but he was light-headed at the time' (9)), and the odds are that some degree of her future comfort *will* depend at some point on her son rather than her husband. But the absurd child-centredness expressed in her rhetoric is also acted out in great social detail in scenes representing the home life of the Middletons.

If it is the strategy of the novel to give us, in the John

Dashwoods, a figure of the linear family in all its ruthless
perfection, an efficient money-gathering machine with no
spare familial parts or vestigial benevolent impulses to retard
its progress, it gives us in the Middletons what we may hope to
be a more typical family instance. The family considers itself
sufficiently well-off to be able to honour its kinship with the
surviving female family of Henry Dashwood by offering the
rental of Barton Cottage on attractive terms, and it is relaxed
enough in its principles of economy to entertain frequently –
indeed, more frequently than the Dashwood women find to
their liking.

We are told early on that the Middletons, having adopted
the typical roles of their caste, are a couple of limited
intellectual resources:

> . . . they kept more company of every kind than any other family
> in the neighbourhood. It was necessary to the happiness of both;
> for however dissimilar in temper and outward behaviour, they
> strongly resembled each other in that total want of talent and
> taste which confined their employments, unconnected with such
> as society produced, within a very narrow compass. Sir John was
> a sportsman, Lady Middleton a mother. He hunted and shot,
> and she humoured her children; and these were their only
> resources. Lady Middleton had the advantage of being able to
> spoil her children all the year round, while Sir John's indepen-
> dent employments were in existence only half the time. (32)

On their first meeting with the Dashwoods, the Middletons
bring along their oldest child, a boy of about six, who provides
a substitute for rational conversation:

> . . . there was one subject always to be recurred to by the ladies
> in case of extremity, for they had to inquire his name and age,
> admire his beauty, and ask him questions which his mother
> answered for him, while he hung about her and held down his
> head, to the great surprise of her ladyship, who wondered at his
> being so shy before company as he could make noise enough at
> home.

His usefulness leads the narrator to observe: 'On every formal
visit a child ought to be of the party, by way of provision for
discourse' (31).

In the Middleton home the children are the centre of attention. Austen spares us the full effect of family life as a child-centred hell until the arrival of Lucy and Nancy Steele for a protracted visit, so that she can register crucial differences between Elinor and Lucy through their reactions to the children. Lucy and Nancy pay court to Lady Middleton through her children, and she accepts their compliments as the most natural of tributes:

> She saw with maternal complacency all the impertinent incroachments and mischievous tricks to which her cousins submitted. She saw their sashes untied, their hair pulled about their ears, their work-bags searched, and their knives and scissors stolen away, and felt no doubt of its being a reciprocal enjoyment. It suggested no other surprise than that Elinor and Marianne should sit so composedly by, without claiming a share in what was passing. (120–1)

When her eldest son throws Nancy's pocket handkerchief out the window, Lady Middleton beams, 'John is in such spirits today!' When the second son pinches Nancy's finger, she 'fondly' observes, 'How playful William is!' (121). A slight scratch suffered by Annamaria is treated as such a life-threatening injury that the child learns always to scream and cry for attention. Doody points to the consequences of this episode from Lady Middleton's career of 'child-spoiling':

> The lot of the female is hard enough without her being educated into hysteria and dependency. Taught by the present of sweetmeats for her tears that she is effective when she cries, little Annamaria is already a sad creation of mock sensibility, made 'feminine' to a dangerous point, owing to Lady Middleton's lack of sense in this matter. (xxiii)

The education received by the Middleton sons is equally appropriate. They are being encouraged to exercise their 'spirits' (that psychic commodity Willoughby so clearly has and Edward and Colonel Brandon often lack) through inflicting their wills on dependent female relations. They should graduate easily from their childhood pursuits of stealing handkerchiefs, knives and scissors, untying sashes, pulling hair

and searching work-bags, into the more adult male employ-
ments of begging locks and letters, stealing kisses and hearts,
perhaps even seducing and abandoning helpless women. Just
as Annamaria is being educated into the rules of tyranny
through calculated weakness, the sons are being educated into
an unthinking tyranny through social permission. Austen's
point is not that they are especially ill-behaved (though they
are), but that their behaviour is being reinforced through Lady
Middleton's positive constructions of it. Spirit and playfulness,
we note, are exercised at the expense of subordinates. The
Steele sisters, to choose an appropriate hunting metaphor, are
fair game.

And like the fox, to whom hunters are fond of attributing an
enjoyment of the chase, Lucy and Nancy protest that they love
it. After Annamaria is whisked away to be given marmalade as
a cure for her sad injury, the Dashwood and Steele sisters
guardedly discuss the Middleton family. Nancy says,

> 'And what a charming little family they have! I never saw such
> fine children in my life – I declare I quite doat upon them already,
> and indeed I am always distractedly fond of children.'
>
> 'I should guess so,' said Elinor with a smile, 'from what I have
> witnessed this morning.'
>
> 'I have a notion,' said Lucy, 'you think the little Middletons
> rather too much indulged; perhaps they may be the outside of
> enough; but it is so natural in Lady Middleton; and for my part,
> I love to see children full of life and spirits; I cannot bear them if
> they are tame and quiet.'
>
> 'I confess,' replied Elinor, 'that while I am at Barton Park, I
> never think of tame and quiet children with any abhorrence.'
> (122–3)

Lucy sees Lady Middleton's indulgence of her children as
'natural', an intriguing word when applied to this woman of
chilly elegance who blanches at the vulgarities of her mother.
Her indulgence of the children is no more natural than that of
the Steele sisters, and it has similar social motivations. Just as
they wish to make themselves indispensable in their social role
of guests, and incidentally to advertise their qualifications as
mothers of the future, Lady Middleton is asserting her own

centrality in the social role of mother. The *reductio ad absurdum* of this kind of marriage, in which the actual relationship between husband and wife is of minimal importance compared to their social roles, is played out in the Palmers, whose only intimate interaction seems to be as propagator and breeder. When Mr Palmer insults his mother-in-law Mrs Jennings, she responds with a home truth: 'Aye, you may abuse me as you please . . . you have taken Charlotte off my hands and cannot give her back again. So there I have the whip hand of you.' Far from being affronted, 'Charlotte laughed heartily to think that her husband could not get rid of her; and exultingly said, she did not care how cross he was to her, as they must live together' (112).

Lucy Steele's strategy in dealing with the hegemony of the linear family, from which she is excluded, is to adopt its principles and insinuate herself into it. When with the Middletons, she cultivates the children and through them their mother. She has already secured a secret engagement to Edward Ferrars (still an eldest son) and has hopes of winning over his mother. When Mrs Ferrars changes eldest sons, so does Lucy, and she finally succeeds in winning the mother's favour as well as Robert's hand. It is tempting to speculate that if Lucy had been in the position of Elinor at Norland, she could have seen to it that her ungrateful uncle never even thought of leaving the estate to his babbling infant nephew. Ranged against the politic strategies of Lucy, so successful because they embrace the linear structural principles of her society, we have the politic strategies of Elinor, who, while sometimes playing what Tanner would call a social game, plays a different game, and by different rules.

One brilliant comic scene epitomises both the struggle for precedence among linear families and the strategies through which outsiders must cope with their aggressive territoriality. An argument arises about whether Lady Middleton's middle son William or young Harry Dashwood, nearly the same age and the only one of the disputed pair present, is the taller. 'The parties stood thus', Austen writes, as though she were reporting a parliamentary debate:

The two mothers, though each really convinced that her own son was the tallest, politely decided in favour of the other.

The two grandmothers, with not less partiality, but more sincerity, were equally earnest in support of their own descendant.

Lucy, who was hardly less anxious to please one parent than the other, thought the boys were both remarkably tall for their age, and could not conceive that there could be the smallest difference in the world between them; and Miss Steele, with yet greater address gave it, as fast as she could, in favour of each.

Elinor, having once delivered her opinion on William's side, by which she offended Mrs. Ferrars and Fanny still more, did not see the necessity of enforcing it by any farther assertion; and Marianne, when called on for her's, offended them all, by declaring that she had no opinion to give, as she had never thought about it. (234)

Elinor and Marianne both err socially on behalf of truth, Elinor taking physical accuracy and Marianne emotional honesty as a guide. Elinor possesses powers of 'address' that Marianne holds in disdain, but reserves them for occasions more significant than this.

Elinor plays by rules she has learned as a child of a different kind of marriage, which we must piece together from dim suggestions, because we are given only the most general sense of the former home life of the Henry Dashwoods:

In the society of his nephew and niece, and their children, the old Gentleman's days were comfortably spent. His attachment to them all increased. The constant attention of Mr. and Mrs. Henry Dashwood to his wishes, which proceeded not merely from interest, but from goodness of heart, gave him every degree of solid comfort which his age could receive; and the cheerfulness of the children added a relish to his existence. (3)

We are led to infer differences between Henry Dashwood's first and second marriages, not least from the radically different behaviours of John and his sisters. The first marriage clearly ran along socially prescribed lines, with Henry Dashwood the inheritor of Norland marrying a woman of large fortune, the union producing one male heir. The marriage is structurally perfect, as, we have already noted, is the marriage of his son.

Henry Dashwood's second marriage is an embarrassing excess, which must be imputed to his desire for something – call it love or human companionship – having outlived the institutional necessity of marriage for the conservation, improvement and transmission of property. The scandalous redundancy of the second marriage is signalled both by Mrs Dashwood's having brought with her no financial resources and by its having produced three daughters who would be drains on the estate were it not for the uncle's will and the quick thinking and quicker talking of Fanny. We are allowed to glimpse the human face of the second marriage only through the social interaction of the remaining family group, Mrs Dashwood and her daughters.

Doody's otherwise splendid treatment of mothers, mothering, maternity and matriarchy scants the positive virtues of Mrs Dashwood, even to the extent of including her 'indulgent and self-indulgent' behaviour within its institutional critique. In this she is in line with the critical tradition on the novel, which, as Johnson points out, has ordinarily seen Mrs Dashwood as 'an excessively lax parent, little more than one of the girls herself'. Johnson adds, however, that Mrs Dashwood 'actually presides over a remarkable little establishment', the cottage at Barton, which 'has meant something very much like regeneration to the shiftless men who retreat there now and then' (70). In a society characterised by crowded, noisy rooms, vapid, infantile conversation and every variety of scheming, mercenary behaviour, just how the Dashwood family creates this spare haven is worth exploration.

It is easy to understand how Mrs Dashwood has earned her unfavourable critical reputation. Her first thoughts are often idealistic, impetuous and impractical. Where she differs from other mothers in the novel, or in Austen's other novels for that matter, is in her ability to entertain second thoughts, often on the advice of Elinor. Take the matter of the scale of living envisioned by Mrs Dashwood during the removal from Norland to Barton:

> The horses which were left her by her husband, had been sold soon after his death, and an opportunity now offering of disposing of her carriage, she agreed to sell that likewise at the earnest advice of her eldest daughter. For the comfort of her children, had she consulted only her own wishes, she would have kept it; but the discretion of Elinor prevailed. *Her* wisdom too limited the number of their servants to three; two maids and a man, with whom they were speedily provided from amongst those who had formed their establishment at Norland. (26)

Although this passage highlights the prudence of Elinor, it also confirms the persuadibility of Mrs Dashwood, who is willing to discuss matters seriously within her family and to acknowledge practical realities when they are demonstrated. The respect for her daughter's opinion evidenced in the passage is unique among the mother–child relationships depicted, which range between the imperious oppressiveness of Mrs Ferrars and the self-satisfied permissiveness of Lady Middleton, with very little in the middle.

Elinor returns her mother's respect, but she is neither heedless nor contemptuous of her tendency toward imprudent generosity. One of the most complex negotiations in the novel occurs when Marianne informs Elinor that Willoughby has offered the gift of a horse he has bred on his estate. Elinor presents substantial arguments against accepting the gift: that her mother would be forced to buy another horse for a servant to ride in accompanying her, that she would have to hire another servant, that a stable would have to be built, and that the propriety of accepting such a gift 'from a man so little, or at least so lately known to her' (58), would be doubtful. Marianne rejects the argument from propriety, but is finally led to decline the gift precisely on the grounds that her mother would be tempted 'to such imprudent kindness' (59) by her mention of the offer.

A discernible undertone in the episode above demonstrates that Mrs Dashwood is the head of a household that could be thick with ungovernable sibling rivalries. Elinor, her eldest daughter at nineteen, is reserved in her temperament, prone to managing her own emotions, and intent on controlling social situations. Marianne at seventeen consciously models herself upon her mother's more open displays of emotion, coded to correspond with doctrines of sensibility, without seeming yet to have her mother's genuine ease and warmth of personality. The two sisters of marriageable age have yet another sister, Margaret, who at thirteen is almost old enough for serious mischief – think forward to Lydia Bennet at fifteen. That Margaret plays a subordinate role in the family, only occasionally threatening the peace of her older sisters through impishly loose talk, places her in sharp contrast to the behaviour of children in the Middleton household. She may not be so uselessly redundant, then, as generations of critics have claimed. Mrs Dashwood's tact and evenhandedness show in her many confidential conversations with her older daughters, all on topics rich in possibilities for triangulation: Marianne concerned about Elinor's strange reserve in her relations with Edward; Elinor worried by Marianne's unreserve with Willoughby; Marianne wondering that Edward has not visited in the first two weeks of their residence at Barton Cottage; Elinor anxious to know the precise nature of the understanding between Marianne and Willoughby. Mrs Dashwood encourages her daughters' individual confidences in the most extended mother–daughter dialogues represented in all of Austen's works, but never betrays the confidence of one to another.

She also skilfully mediates potential conflicts, such as that which occurs when Marianne has, in Elinor's view, been too forthcoming in her conversation on Willoughby's first visit. When Marianne vehemently objects to this criticism, her mother responds:

> 'My love, . . . you must not be offended with Elinor – she was only in jest. I should scold her myself, if she were capable of wishing to check the delight of your conversation with our new friend.' – Marianne was softened in a moment. (48)

In a single statement Mrs Dashwood has turned aside the sharpness of Elinor's remark, silently cautioned Elinor, and adopted Willoughby as 'our' new friend, thus minimising Marianne's self-evident emotional investment in him. As a result of Mrs Dashwood's psychological tact, her small cottage has more room for individual lives, provides as much of what we might now call psychic space, as any of Austen's great houses ever will.

Johnson terms Mrs Dashwood's authority 'entirely non-coercive' (70), a formulation more just than the customary 'indulgent' or 'permissive'. There exists in the household a fair measure of freedom without undue liberties, of permissible difference without antagonism, of order without compulsion. We are always aware of sibling tensions in the family, but we only realise how successfully they are contained and diverted when we see the struggle for primacy which divides other sibling pairs, particularly Lucy and Nancy Steele and Edward and Robert Ferrars. While other heads of families think linearly, in terms of rank, priority and temporality, Mrs Dashwood, concerned more with the present than the past or future, thinks laterally. She is most concerned to make her home a pleasant space for family and friends at a given moment. She graciously entertains three men who are apparently suitors for her daughters without placing them under the slightest pressure. We can only imagine the contrast with Sir John Middleton's and Mr Palmer's prenuptial visits to the daughters of Mrs Jennings, and we do not have to imagine the contrast with eligible males who happen within the reach of Mrs Bennet in *Pride and Prejudice*.

Sense and Sensibility portrays social life as a collision between linear concerns (finding a husband, establishing a family, securing the future) and lateral concerns (savouring the present, assuring sociability, behaving justly and equitably). Although its clear preference is for the latter, in which Mrs Dashwood's and Elinor's actions are quite similar, whatever their differences in temperamental style, it offers neither option as a self-sufficient ideal. While Mrs Dashwood allows her daughters the freedom to grow and learn, she also offers them the opportunity to make dreadful mistakes, as Marianne almost does. Her disdain for the business of marriage is forthright: '*catching*' men, she tells Lord Middleton, 'is not an employment to which . . . [her daughters] have been brought up. Men are very safe with us, let them be ever so rich' (44). When set against the calculating manipulations of Mrs Ferrars or even the better-natured intrigues of Mrs Jennings, Mrs Dashwood's attitude is refreshing. But it also betrays an absence of worldly concern that threatens exposure to her daughters.

On balance, then, *Sense and Sensibility* embraces the implicit social model found in Mrs Dashwood's idea of the family: a group of friends concerned more with living equitably and harmoniously in the present than with projecting themselves and their line into futurity. Nightmarish difficulties beset that uneasy confederation of linear families which gathers in the end around Mrs Ferrars: Lucy and Robert Ferrars, we are told,

> settled in town, received very liberal assistance from Mrs. Ferrars, were on the best terms imaginable with the [John] Dashwoods; and setting aside the jealousies and ill-will continually subsisting between Fanny and Lucy, in which their husbands of course took a part, as well as the frequent domestic disagreements between Robert and Lucy themselves, nothing could exceed the harmony in which they all lived together. (377)

The mode of living among the economically less fortunate members of the Dashwood family stands in stark contrast:

> Mrs. Dashwood was prudent enough to remain at the cottage, without attempting a removal to Delaford; and fortunately for Sir John and Mrs. Jennings, when Marianne was taken from them, Margaret had reached an age highly suitable for dancing, and not very ineligible for being supposed to have a lover.
>
> Between Barton and Delaford, there was that constant communication which strong family affection would naturally dictate; – and among the merits and the happiness of Elinor and Marianne, let it not be ranked as the least considerable, that though sisters, and living almost within sight of each other, they could live without disagreement between themselves, or producing coolness between their husbands. (380)

The keen sense of propriety exhibited by Mrs Dashwood is itself a kind of politics: mothering without smothering, flexibly allowing additional space for the individual lives of her married daughters. After having visited repeatedly to encourage propinquity to do its work for Colonel Brandon upon Marianne, she withdraws to a civil distance: 'constant communication' may be dictated by 'strong family affection' (380), but neither requires nor is nurtured by constant presence. Placed in the context of other sibling relationships in the novel, the claim of amity between Elinor and Marianne is almost utopian in its force. This is not a bad model for social cohesion – for a family, for a community, or for a nation. But it must be created, perhaps even created daily, and it cannot be inherited. It cannot be predicated on the past, nor can it be sublimated for the sake of the future.

6

Constitutional Groundings

It has become a truism of criticism that the literature of the romantic period is riddled with epistemological anxiety. In this it clearly displays its roots in enlightenment thought, whatever its counter-enlightenment tendencies. The remarkable success of empirical philosophy had made it possible to account for human knowledge through individual experience without recourse to principles of innateness. While this epistemological revolution led in literature to an enormous privileging of individual experience, which we see vividly throughout the lyric poetry of the age, it had its darker, shadow side as well. Normally, the literary uncertainties of the age have been traced philosophically, with writers depicted as in a quest to accept what we might call truths of experience while retaining, or perhaps recovering, some basis for transcendental Truth. Indeed, we have been overwhelmed for the better part of a century with studies of William Wordsworth's and Samuel Taylor Coleridge's empiricism and/or transcendentalism, Percy Bysshe Shelley's scepticism and/or Platonism, and the like. Most frequently these studies have narrowed their focus to deal with a narrow case of human knowledge, pitting the individual mind against the universe. If concentration on metaphysics has until recently diminished interest in the social thought of the romantic poets, it has equally marginalised the works of Austen as products of their age, because the individual search for immutable truth is obviously not the stuff of her fiction.

One recent study, Regina Hewitt's *Wordsworth and the*

Empirical Dilemma (1990), suggests a useful redirection of our literary enquiries by asking that we attend to the social as well as the individual consequences of the triumph of empiricism. The potential for solipsism in the new philosophy imperilled not just man's connection with the absolute but also his connection with his fellow man. With political as well as spiritual understandings shaken by the great events in France, the decades bracketing the turn of the century witnessed an avid search for certainty in the grounds of human relationships. Criticism of Austen has recently addressed this phenomenon through its careful attention to issues of human perspective in her works, noting how differently characters perceive and understand events and how much difficulty they have in sharing their understandings. It has pursued in detail the aesthetic consequences of perspectival thinking in Austen's command of point of view. *Emma*, as L. J. Swingle has observed, provides a classic instance of this perspectival comedy of misunderstandings, and he has noted the tendency of characters in the novels to develop into opposing 'parties', grouping themselves into small bands of friends who see the world similarly and recreating on their small scale the party-ridden spirit of the larger social order (see 'The perfect happiness' and 'The poets').

Retrospectively viewing his immersion in social theorising in the first half of the decade, through which he had attempted to account for the bad turn of the Revolution in France and to salvage a hope for human progress from its ruins, William Wordsworth gives a vivid description of a mind tormented by the need for social assurance:

> Thus I fared,
> Dragging all passions, notions, shapes of faith,
> Like culprits to the bar, suspiciously
> Calling the mind to establish in plain day
> Her titles and her honours, now believing,
> Now disbelieving, endlessly perplexed
> With impulse, motive, right and wrong, the ground
> Of moral obligation – what the rule,
> And what the sanction – till, demanding proof,

And seeking it in every thing, I lost
All feeling of conviction, and, in fine,
Sick, wearied out with contrarieties,
Yielded up moral questions in despair,
And for my future studies, as the sole
Employment of the inquiring faculty,
Turned towards mathematics, and their clear
And solid evidence.
(The Prelude [1805], 10:888–904)

Although Wordsworth's epistemological and ethical anxieties are often attributed to a brief adherence to the theories of William Godwin, the terms in which he presents his crisis, with his 'thirst of a secure intelligence' (10:833) leading to a disdain for nature as it is reflected in 'custom', 'written law', 'sundry moral sentiments' (852–3), and 'old opinions' (861), also recalls the broader dimensions of the constitutional debate of the era.

Burke and Paine may continue to serve as representatives of this conflict, here shifted from the discourse of political behaviour to the discourse of political philosophy, not how we should act, but how we may know. For Burke, as for Wordsworth in his reconstruction of his crisis, the only sure anchor is nature, meaning the collective wisdom of human experience. Our institutions and practices have come into being through a glacially slow process of preservation and refinement, and we throw out the smallest examples of human practice at our peril. What Wordsworth's theoretical turn disrupted was his moral heritage, his hereditary stock of cultural understandings. He wished to shake off the

accidents, of nature, time, and place,
That make up the weak being of the past,
Build social freedom on its only basis:
The freedom of the individual mind,
Which to the blind restraints of general laws
Superior, magisterially adopts
One guide – the light of circumstances, flashed
Upon an independent intellect.
(10:822–9)

As this pull between tradition and analytic reason was played out between Burke and Paine, it took the form of a debate about the proper grounds for establishing 'social freedom', which in large part was a debate about the mode of expression and transmission of political culture.

For Burke certainty lies in convention, which is the cumulative product of a series of governmental transactions, such as the Magna Carta, of common law legal decisions resting on precedent, and of customary usages, which may or may not be written. Indeed, the full force of both Burke's and Wordsworth's senses of tradition lies, as James K. Chandler has echoed J. G. A. Pocock in observing, in its being incapable of being written. The 'constitution' of England, its grounds of certainty as a nation, is the more real and the more secure for its *not* being a written document (Chandler 159–60). Paine will have none of this, but insists:

> A constitution is not a thing in name only, but in fact. It has not an ideal, but a real existence; and wherever it cannot be produced in a visible form, there is none. A constitution is a thing *antecedent* to a government, and a government is only the creature of a constitution. The constitution of a country is not the act of its government, but of the people constituting a government.
>
> It is the body of elements, to which you can refer, and quote article by article; and contains the principles on which the government shall be established, the manner in which it shall be organised, the powers it shall have, the mode of elections, the duration of parliaments, or by what other name such bodies may be called; the powers which the executive part of the government shall have; and, in fine, every thing that relates to the complete organization of a civil government, and the principles on which it shall act, and by which it shall be bound. (309)

Because Burke can produce no such document for England, Paine argues, it has no constitution, and its citizens have no grounds of security.

In describing this contest between orality and writing, general understanding and finite obligation, we might seem to have come a considerable distance from the world Austen creates in *Sense and Sensibility*. However, that violation of oral authority which sets the novel in motion – John Dashwood's disregard for his father's dying request – is only the first of a series of complex presentations of the difficulties of arriving at any sense of human security, any constituting foundation for social obligation. Indeed, if there is one observation about the world of this novel on which criticism is agreed, however it understands the work and however it values it, it is that certainty is very difficult to come by. The language of characters is frequently oblique, communication between them is often obscure and indirect, their behaviour is erratic, and their underlying motivations are indecipherable. Not every character notices that understanding is a struggle, because many believe that their particular perspectives exhaust the repertoire of human possibilities; but those who do try find it to be hard work. In her early essay 'The "Twilight of Probability"', Claudia L. Johnson sketched astutely the struggle for understanding that runs through *Sense and Sensibility* and suggested its philosophical roots in Samuel Johnson's essays dealing with uncertainty and hope.

In what becomes almost a signature episode of the novel, a character will perform a surprising, uncharacteristic action, and then leave another set of characters to puzzle over its meaning. Perhaps the fullest example follows the precipitate departure of Willoughby from the neighborhood of Barton Park. Willoughby says his goodbyes cryptically: 'Mrs. Smith has this morning exercised the privilege of riches upon a poor dependant cousin, by sending me on business to London. I have just received my dispatches, and taken my farewel of Allenham; and by way of exhilaration I am now come to take my farewel of you' (76). That Willoughby is lying will ultimately be revealed, but nothing in his speech suggests that he is misrepresenting the reasons for his abrupt departure. His uncertainty and equivocation about the timing and even the possibility of his return to Devonshire, however, leave the episode shrouded in mystery, which Elinor tries her best to penetrate:

She thought of what had just passed with anxiety and distrust. Willoughby's behaviour in taking leave of them, his embarrassment, and affectation of cheerfulness, and, above all, his unwillingness to accept her mother's invitation, a backwardness so unlike a lover, so unlike himself, greatly disturbed her. One moment she feared that no serious design had ever been formed on his side; and the next that some unfortunate quarrel had taken place between him and her sister; – the distress in which Marianne had quitted the room was such as a serious quarrel could most reasonably account for, though when she considered what Marianne's love for him was, a quarrel seemed almost impossible. (77)

The phrases 'unlike a lover' and 'unlike himself' are most interesting. The first represents a violation of a social construction, carried out in language and behaviour, against which anomalous actions may be measured; the other represents a violation of a projected self-construction, Willoughby as he has appeared to be until now, against which his present behaviour tugs. Elinor and Mrs Dashwood disagree on Willoughby's possible motivations for not eagerly and immediately accepting their invitation to visit in the future with them rather than Mrs Smith. Elinor perceives an unwillingness to accept, while her mother sees an inability to accept. Mrs Dashwood surmises – on no authority other than her reading of Willoughby's character – that Mrs Smith suspects and disapproves 'his regard for Marianne' (78). Finally, Elinor and her mother disagree even on the precise nature of the relationship between Willoughby and Marianne.

Mrs Dashwood assumes that Willoughby and Marianne are secretly engaged. Elinor questions whether they are, and what follows is a significant dispute about means of coming to certain knowledge:

'I want no proof of their affection,' said Elinor; 'but of their engagement I do.'
'I am perfectly satisfied of both.'
'Yet not a syllable has been said to you on the subject, by either of them.'
'I have not wanted syllables where actions have spoken so plainly. Has not his behaviour to Marianne and to all of us, for

at least the last fortnight, declared that he loved and considered her as his future wife, and that he felt for us the attachment of the nearest relation? Have we not perfectly understood each other? Has not my consent been daily asked by his looks, his manner, his attentive and affectionate respect? My Elinor, is it possible to doubt their engagement? How could such a thought occur to you? How is it to be supposed that Willoughby, persuaded as he must be of your sister's love, should leave her, and leave her perhaps for months, without telling her of his affection; – that they should part without a mutual exchange of confidence?'

'I confess,' replied Elinor, 'that every circumstance except *one* is in favour of their engagement; but that *one* is the total silence of both on the subject, and with me it almost outweighs every other.' (79–80)

Mrs Dashwood relies on the language of conventional behaviour, constructing intention not through words but through the total expression of being. Elinor wants language of plain and direct assertion, and, failing that, will be satisfied of the engagement only if it is discovered that Marianne and Willoughby 'correspond'. Under prevailing custom, their writing to one another will be proof of their engagement. Mrs Dashwood replies satirically: 'A mighty concession indeed! If you were to see them at the altar, you would suppose they were going to be married. Ungracious girl! But *I* require no such proof' (80).

Mrs Dashwood looks for truth along a romantic/poetic axis which respects socially symbolic behaviour as superior to words: unparsable cumulative behaviour represents character fully. Elinor works along a rational/prosaic axis and wants declarative language, which can be interpreted and challenged directly. She inherently values written over spoken language. Mrs Dashwood, like Marianne, leans toward Burke's traditional view of social connection and obligation, Elinor toward Paine's demand for putting it in writing. Neither is fully correct, though Elinor's rational scepticism is nearer the truth. Marianne and Willoughby are discovered to correspond, but they are not engaged. Even Elinor's trust in writing must itself finally be grounded upon the conventional usage of written language, and she has underestimated both Marianne's willingness to disregard and Willoughby's willingness to manipulate convention. The actual state of human feelings, and the social obligations which connect one person to another, cannot be determined reliably through behaviour, speech, or writing. In a world without discernible certainties, as Susan Morgan has argued persuasively in *In the Meantime*, one viable guide to social interaction is the pattern followed by Elinor: an alert and sceptical observation of decorum, a suspension of full belief and commitment, which allows truth to emerge in the fullness of time.

Elinor especially must inure herself to living in uncertainty. She becomes the unwilling confidante of Lucy Steele, who reveals her secret engagement to Edward in order to head off what she correctly suspects is the growing regard between them. Elinor reluctantly accepts Lucy's veracity after a display of trophies, including of course letters from Edward to her. These establish the literal truth of her engagement, but Lucy's need to display them suggests the shaky nature of the emotional commitment. Elinor must thereafter attend to what Edward says, but even more to what he does not say, and she determines correctly that while he may indeed be caught, he is no longer captivated by Lucy. Language becomes a screen, behind which people may hide but through which they may also communicate.

Perhaps the ultimate corruption of language in the novel occurs when Willoughby returns the letters and lock of hair he has received from Marianne with a covering letter which Elinor describes as 'impudently cruel': a letter which, 'instead of bringing with his desire of a release any professions of regret, acknowledged no breach of faith, denied all particular affection whatever – a letter of which every line was an insult, and which proclaimed its writer to be deep in hardened villany' (184). Such would seem to be the character of Willoughby, set before us in writing, except that we learn in Willoughby's final interview with Elinor that the letter was originally written by his bride-to-be, and he was forced 'servilely' (328) to copy and sign it in order to protect the economic salvation to come from his marriage. Willoughby argues that the actual facts of the situation lessen his guilt. Elinor agrees that they prove his heart 'less wicked, much less wicked'. But, she adds, 'I hardly know – the misery that you have inflicted – I hardly know what could have made it worse' (329–30). Willoughby shares the major characteristic of the novel's users and abusers of custom: they lay claim to the truth of the spirit; but finally, when self-interest is at stake, they live by the letter. John Dashwood claims patrimonial privilege and authority while committing sins of omission that express filial impiety; Lucy Steele flaunts Edward Ferrars's letters as legalistic proof of their engagement while knowing that the affection they expressed has vanished; Willoughby's affair with Eliza and romance with Marianne violated no pledges, because he made none; even Edward, though less consciously manipulative and less culpable than the others, manages stumblingly to conduct a romantic relationship with Elinor while engaged to Lucy through the simple expedient of silence, never expressing his regard for Elinor directly in either speech or writing.

We might sum up the problem of language and certainty in *Sense and Sensibility* in the following way: conventional behaviour and conventional language are woefully inadequate guides to human intention. John Dashwood shallowly emulates the language and action of the provident and benevolent gentry while pursuing a steady course of self-interest. Willoughby, much more adept at disguising his intention, enacts the role of the perfect suitor for Marianne's hand. The problem is that the perfect suitor and the perfect seducer act identically, at least up to a point their relationship never reaches, and an imposture so successful offers no handle on individual intention. Direct privileged communication, such as Lucy's to Elinor, provides no security, because it may be a tissue of half-truths and untruths. Writing is equally subject to deceptive practices, and like conversation it is subject to interpretation. Edward's letters to Lucy are evidence of a secret engagement, but tell nothing of how he currently feels about it. While the novel explores the range of possibilities for grounding social relationships, it finds all of them inadequate to humanity's gifts for deception and self-deception. It is in this stern acceptance of the possibility of successful deceit that Austen differs so much from her predecessor Fanny Burney, who covers much of the same territory. Something in Evelina Anville's nature or upbringing always warns her when someone is false, and she is shaken to the foundations of her being when she receives a letter from Lord Orville that seems to reveal him as dishonourably forward in seeking a secret correspondence with her. When it is discovered that the impertinent letter is a counterfeit, Evelina's and her readers' faith in our ability to penetrate evil is restored. Not so, Austen would comment: liars are better than that.

All this suggests why the conclusions of Austen's novels avoid positing reunited communities, whether founded on custom, as Burke would have it, or law, as Paine advocated. The valued community which forms at the end of this novel constitutes itself across generational lines, with mother and daughters maintaining non-hierarchical attitudes of mutual respect, and across class lines, with Colonel Brandon and Edward, patron and patronised, living as friends and equals. The foundation for these relationships is neither traditional nor contractual, but an intimate knowledge of character, of habitual probity of language and behaviour, tested over time. Genuinely satisfying and nurturing society exists as an enclave rather than an institutional entity; it depends on a location in which happiness can be ordered through mutual effort, not upon a structure which will create order and happiness (on Austen's endings see also Swingle, 'Perfect happiness'; Ruoff, 'Anne Elliot's dowry').

7

Movement and Plot

Having devoted considerable attention to exploring mechanisms of descent in *Sense and Sensibility* – literally, with respect to the transmission of property and wealth, figuratively with respect to the role played by social and political principles of linearity – I will close this reading with two sections on Austen's relationship to her literary heritage, how she found the estate of fiction and how she left it. The vocabulary of inheritance – heritage, tradition, legacy, patrimony – remains almost as politically volatile today as it was in Austen's time, but it has migrated to the sphere of intellectual, artistic and cultural life. This language is central to the 'canon debate' in the United States, where on one side we see proponents of something like a great tradition, arguing that literature in English is an entailed inheritance, which must be transmitted whole, entire and unquestioned to future generations, and on the other side we see various improvers, usually proponents of contemporary theory, arguing that received literary history is a social and intellectual construct with the purpose not of conserving the best that has been thought and written but of excluding anything that bearers of privilege find discomforting. While any critic of Austen should be uncomfortable arguing against the existence and importance of literary greatness, my reading has attempted to demonstrate that *Sense and Sensibility* has been relatively ignored – at least received and written about less glowingly than *Pride and Prejudice* and *Emma* – precisely because it is so profoundly and radically critical of received social principles. While the tendency of

Austen's 'politics' may still be legitimately contested, her aesthetic stance is clear: she is a lifelong inveterate improver of the estate of fiction, lovingly aware of the deficits of literary tradition and committed to remaking the novel. There may be somewhere a writer who believes that while the stories through which society constructs itself need radical amendment, the society itself is sound and whole. But I have never read such a writer.

I mentioned near the outset of this reading that *Sense and Sensibility* structures itself according to the physical movement of characters. The death of Henry Dashwood and the passage of the estate to his son John create the need for the Dashwood women to seek a new residence. Their removal from Norland Park in Sussex to Barton Cottage in Devonshire brings a new set of acquaintances, the opportunity to see old acquaintances in altered circumstances, and a new physical, social and economic environment. The middle third of the narrative traces the travels of Elinor and Marianne to other unfamiliar environments, first as house-guests of Mrs Jennings in London, then of the Palmers at Cleveland in Somersetshire. The final movement returns the sisters first to Barton and then to their neighbouring marital destinations, the mansion-house and parsonage at Delaford. In their travels Elinor and Marianne encounter hostility and betrayal, and Marianne suffers a near brush with death.

Expressed so abstractly, the scheme of action of *Sense and Sensibility* seems the very stuff of Western narrative – heroic, cultural and educational journeying which can be traced to the Bible, *The Odyssey* and *Gilgamesh*, and which forms the narrative core of bourgeois romance, the novel as it takes form in England in the century before Austen. Elinor and Marianne are distant cousins of an easily discernible line of road warriors: Christian, Robinson Crusoe, Moll Flanders, Gulliver, Joseph Andrews, Tom Jones, Peregrine Pickle, Caleb Williams, and countless others. Even to name this lineage, of course, is to see Austen's deviations from it. Psychologically arduous as the Dashwood sisters' travels are, they are confined to the inland south of England, unexposed to such exotics as pirates, high-waymen and Scots, and they encounter a narrow spectrum of upper-middle-class characters with behaviours ranging no further afield than the amiable vulgarity of Mrs Jennings and the hostile formality of Mrs Ferrars. Within the context of eighteenth-century fiction, the Dashwood girls are not expansive travellers, and Austen knew it.

Austen's extreme curtailment of movement in her fiction is best seen through her further revision of Fanny Burney's already revisionary treatment of the topic. Burney prefaced *Evelina* (1778) with a disclaimer that will be repeated by writers as different as Maria Edgeworth, Walter Scott and Austen herself: 'Let me . . . prepare for disappointment those who, in the perusal of these sheets, entertain the gentle expectation of being transported to the fantastic regions of Romance, where Reason is an outcast, and where the sublimity of the Marvellous rejects all aid from sober Probability' (8). Her educative journey moves Evelina Anville through a range of contemporary environments: Berry Hill, the home of her sequestered upbringing; the great estate of Howard Grove; the high life and low life of London; and the resorts of Bristol and Bath. In Evelina's travels she is always in the company of a chaperone, some much more assiduous and worthy than others. Still, she is semi-kidnapped by lecherous titled admirers, subjected to threats of physical assault, and brought into close contact with characters representing extremes of the social and moral scales. Madame Duval, her exquisitely vulgar grandmother, has been a long-time resident of France, and runs foul of Captain Mirvan, a bluff English francophobe who stages a mock robbery of the carriage in which Evelina and she are riding, all for the good fun of trussing up the old lady and rolling her in a ditch. Mr Mcartney is a mysterious starving Scots poet who believes that he has fallen in love with his half-sister and attempted to murder his father. He turns out instead to be the half-brother of Evelina, while the young lady with whom he is in love is revealed to be the child of Evelina's first nurse, passed off on Evelina's estranged father, Lord Belmont, as herself. For Austen, Burney's version of 'probability' is itself improbable.

Throughout her career Austen played parodically with the travel motif of her fictive heritage, including the works of Burney. *Love and Freindship* had riotous fun with the astonishing mobility of her roguish teenagers, who leave London for Scotland at a moment's notice, and with less than a moment's thought. The autobiography of its heroine Laura sounds like the daydream of a housebound map-gazer: 'My Father was a native of Ireland & an inhabitant of Wales; My Mother was the natural Daughter of a Scotch Peer by an italian Opera-girl – I was born in Spain & received my Education at a Convent in France' (6:77). *Emma*, the story of Austen's most prominent intellectual shut-in, organises itself around such fearsome journeys as a half-mile drive on Christmas Eve from Hartfield to Randalls, with the party cut short by the terror generated by a light snowfall. To Emma, of course, the return trip, in which she is subjected to unexpected and unwanted professions of love from the Rev. Mr Elton, is long enough indeed. And that surely is Austen's point: that adventures which baffle expectations, challenge the soul, and provide new openings on the phenomenon of human character can and do happen everywhere.

Still, lusting for adventurous narrative, even Austen's intimate audience of friends and family kept asking for more. She sketched a plot she called 'Plan of a Novel, According to Hints from Various Quarters', in response to their suggestions. Here is a small portion of the projected adventure:

> Heroine & her Father never above a fortnight together in one place, *he* being driven from his Curacy by the vile arts of some totally unprincipled & heart-less young Man, desperately in love with the Heroine, & pursuing her with unrelenting passion – no sooner settled in one Country of Europe than they are necessitated to quit it & retire to another – always making new acquaintance, & always obliged to leave them. ... At last, hunted out of civilised Society, denied the poor Shelter of the humblest Cottage, they are compelled to retreat into

Kamschatka, where the poor Father, quite worn down, finding his end approaching, throws himself on the Ground, & after 4 or 5 hours of tender advice & parental Admonition to his miserable Child, expires in a fine burst of Literary Enthusiasm, intermingled with Invectives again[st] Holders of Tythes. – Heroine inconsolable for some time – but afterwards crawls back towards her former Country – having at least 20 narrow escapes of falling into the hands of Anti-hero – & at last in the very nick of time, turning a corner to avoid him, runs into the arms of the Hero himself. (6:429–30)

Given Austen's continuing critique of adventure as the basis of fiction, which continues intact from the broad parody of her juvenilia through the muted reflexive perfection of *Emma*, we may safely suspect that travel and movement in the novels are never wholly innocent. In *Sense and Sensibility* they are heavily gendered concepts.

Fiction which turns on action depends upon agency: action can represent character because it proceeds from choice, and human choices express ethical leanings and spiritual yearnings. Choice, agency and mobility are important issues in *Sense and Sensibility* because the novel divides these topics along axes of wealth and gender. The world is not all before the Dashwood women because their freedom of choice and movement are restricted. No situation in the neighbourhood of Norland Park answers simultaneously the family's 'notions of comfort and ease' (14) and the constraints of its income. The removal to Barton Cottage in Devonshire is initiated by a proposal from Sir John Middleton, which the family has the power only to decline or to accept. Even their means of mobility, horses and carriage, must be sacrificed in the interest of economy, just as Willoughby's later offer of a horse for Marianne must be declined. To the degree that movement is the token of volition, the Dashwood women have been deprived of the outward symbol of their wills.

The book remains remarkably true to this pattern of action. Although Sir John generously offers the Dashwoods the use of his carriage, 'the independence of Mrs. Dashwood's spirit overcame the wish of society for her children; and she was resolute in declining to visit any family beyond the distance of a walk' (40). The world in which the women move at Barton is contained within a circumference of about a mile and a half. Any movement beyond this perimeter is dependent on others of greater mobility, which translates to different gender or greater means. A twelve-mile excursion to Whitwell, the estate of a brother-in-law of Colonel Brandon, is the grandest adventure planned in their early days in their new residence. That outing requires the intervention of Colonel Brandon to gain access to the house and grounds, along with the co-operation of Sir John and Willoughby in arranging transportation in open carriages. When that trip has to be aborted because of the mysterious letter Colonel Brandon receives, Willoughby gives Marianne the consolation prize of an unchaperoned surreptitious visit to Allenham, his aunt's estate, in her absence.

Throughout the novel the movements of the Dashwood women are subject to the wills of others. Elinor and Marianne travel to London at the invitation of Mrs Jennings. While they are in London, they spend the bulk of their time accompanying her on shopping expeditions and visits to her friends. When Mrs Palmer's child is born, Mrs Jennings spends much of her time with them, and Marianne and Elinor are compelled to spend their days with the Middletons, who have as their houseguests the Steele sisters. When Mrs Jennings accompanies her daughter and grandchild back to Cleveland, the Dashwood sisters are also invited, and accept because it will make their return to Barton less difficult and expensive. All movement by Elinor and Marianne is governed by invitation, the need for economy and the observation of proper decorum for young ladies. They have limited power to decline action, and almost none to initiate it.

Standing in stark contrast is the pattern of masculine movement in the novel. The unmarried males – Willoughby, Edward and Colonel Brandon – are all marked by sudden appearances and sudden departures. Willoughby, as we have already noted, proclaims unexpectedly that he must leave Devonshire immediately on business for Mrs Smith. Colonel

Brandon suddenly interrupts the outing to Whitwell because he has been called away on urgent business. Edward comes and goes in no predictable pattern, even though he has no regular business at all. The lives of Marianne and Elinor are conducted in a constricted space, whether that space at any given moment is Barton Cottage, London or Cleveland, and their lives are intersected by those of the male characters moving in much larger orbits in response to motivations to which the sisters are not privy. To those whose lives are led under such constraints, men's actions can be observed only partially, and they are mysterious.

The narrative device which expresses this mystery most fully is the sudden reappearance which defeats expectations. Shortly after Willoughby has left Devonshire, Marianne sees a 'man on horseback' (86) approaching and is certain it must be Willoughby. It turns out to be Edward, who is equally unexpected. After Marianne and Elinor arrive in London, Marianne writes to Willoughby and constantly expects his arrival. A knock at the door leads Marianne to exclaim, 'Oh! Elinor, it is Willoughby, indeed it is!' (161), only to have Colonel Brandon appear. While Elinor and Lucy are involved in one of their tensely triangulated conversations about Lucy's engagement to Edward, he suddenly appears himself at Elinor's door, to the confusion and consternation of all three. While Elinor is painfully writing to Edward to inform him of the living Colonel Brandon is offering him, Edward appears unexpectedly at Mrs Jennings's house. At Cleveland when Marianne's life is in danger, Colonel Brandon dashes off to bring Mrs Dashwood to her daughter's sick-bed. Elinor sits up alone expecting their arrival. A carriage arrives in great haste, and Elinor 'rushed forward towards the drawing-room, – she entered it, – and saw only Willoughby' (316). Finally, after Elinor has been persuaded that Edward and Lucy are married, she sees another man on horseback she takes to be Colonel Brandon, but who turns out to be Edward, who reveals that Lucy has actually married his younger/older brother Robert. (For further consideration of the implications of mistaken identity in the novel, see Miller 66–77.)

Coincidence and unexpected appearances were as much the stock-in-trade of the popular fiction of Austen's day as they are of ours, and she spoofed these narrative devices mercilessly in her juvenile works. In *Sense and Sensibility*, however, the devices are given structural importance and thematic resonance. Male characters have mobility, which gives them obvious power of agency. Their greater independence of movement reflects far greater independence of will, and their actions are not easily understood by the women whose lives they impact upon so profoundly. For this reason considerably more attention is given in the novel to the interpretation of action than to its depiction. Women hazard guesses about the motivations of men based upon their limited opportunities to observe them. But pondering why Edward is moody, why Colonel Brandon must leave Barton, and why Willoughby acts so strangely upon his departure will never reveal the truth behind their actions, because information which could clarify and explain is simply withheld from the female characters as well as the reader. When men are absent, their actions are unaccountable, unless they choose to account for them.

Sense and Sensibility, then, is a travel novel with a difference. While it is structured around the geographical movements of Elinor and Marianne, it does not suggest that those actions are in themselves the things that form or reveal character. London and Cleveland simply offer different environments in which their behaviour may be circumscribed. Rather than allowing this phenomenon to deny women the power of moral agency, Austen uses it to generate a different understanding and valuation of action itself. Sir Walter Scott, one of our best early readers of Austen, was the first critic to remark tellingly on the lack of 'story' in Austen's fiction. In his 1815 review of *Emma*, he rehearses the plot of the novel and then comments: 'Such is the simple plan of a story which we peruse with pleasure, if not with deep interest, and which we might perhaps more willingly resume than one of those narratives where the attention is strongly riveted, during the first perusal, by the powerful excitement of curiosity' (*CH1* 67). Any of the embedded tales in *Sense and Sensibility* – Colonel Brandon's account of his sad early life and travels, Willoughby's confession of his seduction of Eliza, love for Marianne and marriage to Miss Gray, Edward's revelation of his alienation from his family and infatuation with and unfortunate engagement to Lucy – has inherently more 'story' to it, more action, greater variety of scene and incident, and more plot than the lives of Elinor and Marianne.

Although it is not presented with this intention, our best account of Austen's revision of the concepts of action and agency in *Sense and Sensibility* is the chapter devoted to the novel in Stuart Tave's *Some Words of Jane Austen*, the most significant portion of which tracks scrupulously the 'exertions' of Elinor (74–115). 'Exertion' is a very physical word for such a drawing-room-bounded novel, and it is clear that Austen has chosen it to redefine both the site and nature of moral action and the idea of heroism itself. Our best example is a scene in which Elinor does much while nothing seems to happen. The episode occurs in Mrs Jennings's house in London, where Lucy has sought out Elinor to preen herself over the success of her introduction to Mrs Ferrars, who was 'exceedingly affable' (239) to her while snubbing and insulting Elinor. Just after Lucy has hypocritically proclaimed the support she finds in Elinor's friendship, her 'greatest comfort . . . next to Edward's love' (240), Edward is unexpectedly admitted to this private conference between his fiancée and his beloved. As Austen puts it, 'It was a very awkward moment; and the countenance of each shewed that it was so. They all looked exceedingly foolish' (240). But this narrow moment allows Elinor ample opportunity to exhibit her capacity for meaningful action.

Those actions, which take place on the smallest of scales, consist primarily in Elinor's efforts to control her language and expression:

> . . . she forced herself, after a moment's recollection, to welcome
> him, with a look and manner that were almost easy, and almost
> open; and another struggle, another effort still improved them.
> She would not allow the presence of Lucy, nor the consciousness
> of some injustice towards herself, to deter her from saying that
> she was happy to see him, and that she had very much regretted
> being from home, when he called before in Berkeley-street. She
> would not be frightened from paying him those attentions
> which, as a friend and almost a relation, were his due, by the
> observant eyes of Lucy, though she soon perceived them to be
> narrowly watching her. (241)

The vigour of Austen's language ('forced', 'struggle', 'effort',
'frightened') conveys the difficulties Elinor undergoes in maintaining the appearance of ordinariness. Elinor's most trying
action, however, is a physical movement that goes beyond the
business of composing herself and making Edward as comfortable as she can:

> Her exertions did not stop here; for she soon afterwards felt
> herself so heroically disposed as to determine, under pretence of
> fetching Marianne, to leave the others by themselves: and she
> really did it, and *that* in the handsomest manner, for she loitered
> away several minutes on the landing-place, with the most high-
> minded fortitude, before she went to her sister. (241–2)

'Exertions', 'fortitude', 'heroic disposition': Austen chooses to
present the simple act of renunciation shown through Elinor's
leaving the room in a language suitable for an endangered
heroine of adventure fiction, or for her courageous rescuer.
True, the passage rings of mock-heroism, and Elinor's com-
placency about the highmindedness of her own heroism does
have its comic side; but Elinor still is performing an act of self-
abnegation of which Lucy would be wholly incapable. In a
scene like this we watch the framework of geographical travel
governing the narrative become little more than an ironic
backdrop to highlight the restricted space and attenuated
action through which meaningful human effort can actually be
represented. The arena of heroism is not a distant time or
place; it is always where we are, and always now.

Austen's deployment of motifs of travel and action in *Sense and Sensibility* turns the novel into a double-edged critique of traditional fictional emplotment. It uses for its framework a familiar narrative form which normally equates significant movement with geographical displacement and meaningful moral action with exciting incident. Despite the adventures of Moll Flanders and the peregrinations of more recent gothic heroines, as presented by writers of both sexes, this form has been based on largely masculine principles of action: Austen must undermine and revise it in order to reveal the significance of the lives which women characteristically lead. It is a start, but hardly enough, for Fanny Burney to have an Evelina threatened with sexual assault in the dark walks of an existing Vauxhall Garden, which any Londoner of her day could visit. Burney's roots in picaresque adventure fiction will allow Ann Radcliffe to exoticise the adventures of her own naive heroines, forcing them to show their mettle while being dragged through the mountains of Italy and held captive in the forbidding ruins of ancient castles. With *Evelina* Burney changed the locale of adventure fiction, but not its essential premises. Austen acknowledges, even insists, that a life of adventure is denied to women of the Dashwoods' class. But this denial does not deprive them of the power, or the burden, of moral agency. Nor does the broader range of action and movement allowed men necessarily make their action more significant. In the process of creating a form to represent female agency, Austen also calls into question the adequacy of inherited forms for representing masculine life. Colonel Brandon's heroism is displayed not so much through such stereotypically gendered acts as his duel with Willoughby (which is as eventless as it is pointless) as in his generosity to Edward. Edward's heroism is reflected not in his hapless wanderings but in the quiet integrity with which he resists family tyranny and stands by an engagement he no longer desires but cannot in honour break. Austen's practice in *Sense and Sensibility*, as it is throughout her novels, is to exploit parodically the imbalance between what actually happens and the melodramatic narrative expectations her readers have brought to her fiction. Her most meaningful scenes are often strictly circumscribed, enclosed and almost devoid of overt action. The conflicts represented in them are muted and indirect. Her narrative serves to wean the reader from the enthralment of large-scale schemes of geographical displacement and bold movement.

8

Women's Lives and Men's Stories

Novels depict the movement of characters through both space and time. We have just observed the peculiar spatial construction of *Sense and Sensibility*, in which such basic elements of narrative as distance and mobility are governed by gender-based social and cultural codes. Austen resolves this fictive problem very effectively by writing against the grain, employing traditional spatial motifs while parodically subverting them. Austen's handling of such topics as time and memory, the building blocks of personal history, is equally gendered, but an exploration of its paradoxes suggests how much remains to be done in both Austen's and subsequent novelists' rethinking of narrative strategy. An analysis of temporality in *Sense and Sensibility* – the terms in which the histories of men's and women's lives are represented – becomes almost necessarily a prolepsis to an analysis of temporality in her other mature works, unwritten as well as written at the time of its publication.

Early in this reading I attempted briefly to reconstruct some emotional history of the Dashwood family that might explain why the characters of John Dashwood and his half-sisters are so radically different. This effort was possible only through the assumption that structural differences in the two marriages of Henry Dashwood reflected emotional differences in the husband–wife relationships and generated different behavioural patterns in the progeny of the marriages. Such a tissue of inference was necessary because no single event from either marriage is ever represented, or even recollected, in the novel.

(John's mother is in fact described only through her financial assets.) The exposition with which the fiction begins establishes in detail the social and economic situation of the women protagonists, but it does nothing to explain their psychological make-up. Mrs Dashwood's warmth and generosity, Elinor's candour and prudence and Marianne's romantic impetuosity come to us as given attributes. We are able to accept them with little question because they are plausible differentiae among mothers and daughters, younger and older siblings; but nothing in the novel itself points to how their characters were formed, and nothing in their recollected pasts reflects in any way on their present actions. Their characters are wholly contained within and conveyed through the events of the several months represented in the novel.

Austen's narrative practice, in which a novel is devoted to what Aristotle might have called the narration of a complete action rather than a life history, is part of what we ordinarily think of as the progress of the novel. The roots of the English novel are arguably found in a seamy and shapeless sub-literature of life histories, pseudo-biographies and pseudo-confessions of highwaymen, whores and wanderers, which are clearly visible in the works of Daniel Defoe. The most significant earlier attempts to achieve independent aesthetic shape for the genre were Henry Fielding's invocation of the epic model in *Tom Jones* and Samuel Richardson's invention of the novel in letters. Richardson's example might be viewed as a lyrical model, allowing for greater narrative compression, emotional intensity, individualised expression and dramatic tension than was characteristic of the first-person retrospective narration practised by Defoe. Despite her comic bent, and undoubtedly as a consequence of Fanny Burney's serio-comic adaptation of the Richardsonian model, Austen was drawn more to the intensity of Richardson than to the sweep of Fielding. Her mature narrative method evolved from her fledgling efforts as a writer of epistolary fiction.

Two factors combine to create the marked temporal compression of *Sense and Sensibility*. Austen's interest in protracted individual scenes, presenting character through small nuances of action and language, militates against the expansive representation of time. Her selection of protagonists and their moments of crisis restricts her temporal scope even further. In this novel – indeed in all her novels until *Persuasion* – Austen features young women on the brink of adulthood. Susan Morgan has described two plot types in Austen's mature fiction: 'novels of crisis', including *Northanger Abbey*, *Pride and Prejudice* and *Emma*, in which the heroines must overtly triumph over their intellectual and moral shortcomings; and 'novels of passage', *Sense and Sensibility*, *Mansfield Park* and *Persuasion*, whose heroines 'cannot be described as making the traditional progressive journey from self-deception to understanding' and who 'experience no sudden epiphany which functions as a rite of passage' (Morgan 7). In either case, the temporal focus is a mere span of months, surrounding the heroine's movement from daughterhood to wifehood, from her family by birth to her family by marriage. The typical subject of the novels, then, is the *ingénue*, a character-type whose defining feature is a lack of prior experience. The subtitle Austen's obvious forerunner Fanny Burney gave *Evelina*, 'The History of a Young Lady's Entrance into the World', seems in that work almost literally true. The heroine's upbringing at Berry Hill provided her with principles and predispositions, but no events or experiences: a rendering of a woman's early life uncannily akin to Platonic pre-existence.

In *Sense and Sensibility* these factors combine to create a faithful and telling depiction of the surface temporality, the texture of the lived experience of women's lives: the ennui of frivolous social occasions; the tension of unsought and painful confidences in conversations carried on under the cover of the language of civility; the oppressive burden of time as Marianne waits in London for Willoughby to call, or Elinor waits at Cleveland for Marianne's illness to run its course. What is absent in the novel is any representation of the interpenetration of women's past and present experiences, any suggestion that differing individual responses to a single event are coloured by experiences of the past. Elinor and Marianne, our centres of consciousness in the work, appear in a strange way to have been born yesterday, without histories. While the novel makes fun of Marianne's sentimental credo that a person can truly love only once, it nevertheless conforms to this cultural stricture by presenting us with two heroines who have had no prior romantic experience. Experience within the temporal span of the novel is crucial, while experience before the novel begins is ignored, if not forbidden. And with good reason: in *Lady Susan*, the unpublished epistolary novel of her early maturity, Austen had created a heroine with a past. Lady Susan's history of sexual and economic intrigues is poised throughout against the naive and innocent charm of her daughter Frederica, whom she is trying to force into marriage for money with a titled fool. The novel suggests the degree to which a woman's 'past' is associated with immorality – a linkage which remains current in one the favourite Hollywood plot-lines, wherein the beautiful and apparently ideal wife of a man of substance is discovered to have been – gasp! – a prostitute.

The absence of any representation of the deep past in women's lives unbalances the structure of *Sense and Sensibility*, because the novel relies for its plot complications almost entirely on events which occurred before the action proper of the novel had even begun. The events which generate the clouds of mystery surrounding the three male protagonists – Edward's secret engagement to Lucy, Willoughby's offhand seduction of the second Eliza, and Colonel Brandon's ill-fated love for the first Eliza – all took place before the events on which the novel centres. The novel creates a clear structural divide: while nothing in their pasts clarifies or explains the behaviour of its central female characters, its male characters' behaviours are entirely subject to their pasts, which are unknown and unknowable.

The novel handles its unravelling of these plot complications in as routine a fashion as could be imagined. Each male protagonist is given a confessional scene with Elinor, in which he tells his story, explaining the events which have led him to his fate. In London, Colonel Brandon reveals the history of his love for Eliza – their attachment from childhood; their planned and thwarted elopement; her forced marriage to his brother; his banishment from the parental home and service in India; her fall from virtue, divorce and death after giving birth to her illegitimate daughter. On a cold and stormy night at Cleveland, Willoughby bursts upon Elinor to tell his tale – his regard and love for Marianne thwarted by his habits of expense; his frivolous affair with Colonel Brandon's young ward; his prospects blighted by the stern disapproval of his wealthy relative Mrs Smith, whose inheritance he desperately needs; his loveless marriage to Miss Grey as a means of saving himself from economic ruin and resecuring Mrs Smith's approval. Finally, Edward shows up at Barton Cottage to relate the story of his foolish attachment to Lucy and his miraculous escape therefrom. Contrived and melodramatic as these interpolated narratives are, they lend to the lives of the male protagonists a temporal density notably absent in those of the women.

The fictional form to which *Sense and Sensibility* is closest in its gendering of temporality is Ann Radcliffe's version of the gothic novel, for which the way was paved by Burney's *Evelina*. While holding in disdain the 'sublimity of the Marvellous' and valorising 'sober Probability' (8), Burney nevertheless managed to anticipate in modern-dress many of Radcliffe's gothic terrors and topics. Radcliffe's fiction depended equally upon innocent, unformed and highly impressionable young women to register seismographically the terrors to which they are exposed, and on world-weary, brooding hero/villains, men of mystery haunted by the memory of some heinous crime. Austen's immersion in this form is evidenced by *Northanger Abbey*, which remains the finest spoof of this frequently parodied popular genre. Its impressionable young heroine, Catherine Morland, more naive than even Marianne Dashwood, prowls the forbidden recesses of the abbey for evidence that its owner is tormented by the recollection of some grave crime committed against his late wife, only to discover that while General Tilney is a thoroughly unpleasant man, his failing is plain and simple greed rather than a proclivity for locking up or doing away with wives. The dependance of *Sense and Sensibility* upon a gothic temporal economy suggests that it was easier for Austen to parody the excesses of gothic convention than to erase traces of its influence. Austen has not yet developed more sophisticated ways to attempt to free the representation of women's lives from the hegemony of men's stories. Needless to say, this dilemma of the woman writer did not end with Austen, and there are many who would say that the task can never be completed.

I have discussed elsewhere the cultural importance of temporality in Austen's fiction (Ruoff, 'The triumph of *Persuasion*'). She worked from and against male fictions, one proverbial strain of which insistently differentiates men from women on the basis of their strength of memory. Women are fickle, changeable and inconstant. To cite one renowned example, Alexander Pope's *Moral Essays*, 'Epistle II, To a Lady', begins,

> Nothing so true as what you once let fall,
> 'Most Women have no Characters at all.'
> Matter too soft a lasting mark to bear,
> And best distinguished by black, brown, or fair.

Pope's dominant theme is woman's inconsistency, and the verse letter piles examples one upon another before explaining the formation of admirable female character, like that of the lady Pope is addressing, who is set apart from her sex. However questionable Pope's epistle may seem as theology and moral philosophy, it is superb literary criticism. God may not have created admirable women with a smattering of this and a pinch of that, in defiance of all the dread 'natural' tendencies of their sex, but male fictions surely have. For Pope, woman is 'Matter too soft a lasting mark to bear'. The image recalls John Locke's conception of the mind as tablet upon which experience writes, and whose retentiveness is crucial to the development of all higher moral, intellectual and spiritual powers: no memory, no mind. To grasp the significance of this denial, we need only recollect the privilege of memory in archaic cultures, where the welfare of the tribe depends on exact preservation of rituals; in Platonic epistemology, where anamnesis is the road to truth; in Augustinian theology, where memory and the sacred text converge in the knowledge of God; and of course in Burkean social thought, where fidelity to tradition is of paramount value. Denial of memory to women underpins male hegemony. Any number of Penelopes and Patient Griseldas cannot outweigh the social, political, cultural and economic construct which has rationalised woman's inferiority by proclaiming her inconstancy. From that denial of memory, which suggests that women differ from men as historical beings, proceeds a familiar list of ills, all of which result in the sequestration of women from the processes of history.

No single element in the development of Austen's art may finally be more important than her efforts to resolve the temporal impasse signalled in *Sense and Sensibility*. This achievement will become work of her second period – the final three novels – because the temporal constraints we have noted are even more strictly observed in *Pride and Prejudice*. There the only significant events that antedate the central action of the novel involve the relationship of Wickham to the Darcy family. This complication and clarification is simplicity itself compared with the unearthing of the many buried secrets of *Sense and Sensibility*. No past action by Elizabeth Bennet, our centre of interest in *Pride and Prejudice*, materially affects the plot of the novel. Austen's attempt to resolve the problems of temporality and the representation of female character uncovered in *Sense and Sensibility* begins seriously in *Mansfield Park*. Its fictive time greatly extended, that work becomes more nearly a history of a life than an imitation of an action. Four chapters of summary narration, interspersed with brief scenes and snatches of dialogue, relate the histories of the Misses Ward of Huntingdon, their marriage and progeny, successes and disappointments, the background of the Mansfield family itself, how Fanny Price came at the age of ten to become a dependant of the Sir Thomas Bertrams, and how she passed her first eight years on the estate. The very different narrative strategies of *Mansfield Park* must in some way have proceeded from a limitation sensed in those employed in *Pride and Prejudice*. As Jane Austen told Cassandra on 29 January 1813, she had certainly 'lop't and crop't' that work successfully (*Letters* 298), but she clearly avoids such compression in the following novel. Instead she stretches out the story itself, giving Fanny more space for growth than any other of her heroines and over twice as many separate appearances as Elizabeth Bennet (Kroeber, *Styles in Fictional Structure* 231). The multiplication of scenes calls attention to the continuity within the growth of Fanny's character, creating a field of memory far more extensive than those of the Dashwood or Bennet sisters, whose recollections are severely foreshortened by being limited to reflections on the fictive time-span of the narrative. Fanny is even allowed memories which extend beyond the more expansive bounds of this narrative in her early nostalgia for her brothers and sisters at Portsmouth and, more importantly, in those childhood experiences she relives with her brother William during his visit at Mansfield. With William,

> all the evil and good of their earliest years could be gone over again, and every former united pain and pleasure retraced with the fondest recollection. An advantage this, a strengthener of love, in which even the conjugal tie is beneath the fraternal. Children of the same family, with the same first associations and habits, have some means of enjoyment in their power, which no subsequent connections can supply. (3:234–5)

Stuart Tave has discussed brilliantly the thematic role of memory in *Mansfield Park*, demonstrating conclusively that strength of memory is an index to ethical consistency in the novel (194–204). Fanny is no 'deeper' a character than Elinor Dashwood or Elizabeth Bennet, but Jane Austen's narrative choices in *Mansfield Park* present her more deeply.

Both *Emma* and *Persuasion* return superficially to the

temporal constraints of the earlier works, in that their action proper takes place over a matter of months rather than years. But in both these works the present of the heroines is deeply coloured by their pasts. Emma is surrounded by a host of watchers and rememberers, who are to her mind only too prone to remark on how her current behaviour is reminiscent of that of her earlier years. Mr Knightley is especially given to remembering handsome reading lists compiled but books unread, portraits begun but never finished, all manner of programmes of reform started but never fulfilled. In Anne Elliot of *Persuasion* we are finally given a heroine who is a woman of experience, who at twenty-seven has achieved the precise age that Marianne Dashwood claimed would never allow her 'to hope to feel or inspire affection again' (38), and whose life is lived in the constant memory of a romance which failed seven years before the beginning of the novel. The central clarification scene of the novel is a spirited debate between Anne and Captain Harville about the relative strength of the memories of men and women. When Harville cites the testimony of literature 'upon woman's inconstancy', Anne rejects it: '. . . if you please, no reference to examples in books. Men have had every advantage of us in telling their own story. Education has been theirs in so much higher a degree; the pen has been in their hands. I will not allow books to prove any thing' (5:234).

Viewed from a long perspective, Austen's fictional project was to make books that can prove things, to put the pen into the hands of women by developing formal procedures through which they could tell their own histories, not mutated versions of men's histories. Women's histories are never complete without acknowledgment of the constraints of gender, class and relative economic power, and they cannot finally be told without a remaking of fictional tradition which radically altered our literary heritage. *Sense and Sensibility* offers us entry into the first public step of this process. It is a work which insists that the lives of women are different and require a differently told story. It denaturalises both social and fictive custom, calling attention to the artificiality of systems of action and thought so widespread that they have become transparent. It creates a full social and economic environment for its characters, and its emphasis on the importance of internal response and small-scale actions rather than overt adventure will become a hallmark of most serious fiction over the next two centuries. Its major unresolved problematic, fictive presentation of subtle and complex issues of personal and social history, will preoccupy Austen for the remainder of her brief and brilliant career. It will also become her major legacy to those future novelists, like Virginia Woolf, who have been aware of their heritage. This claim should not be mistaken as further celebration of the internalisation, psychologisation and lyricisation of modern fiction, a critical posture which values that form for all the aspects of life it ignores. What Woolf taught herself was how to centre a social novel around the catastrophe of the Great War, tell it through the intense depiction of two days of life in the Hebrides, and call it *To the Lighthouse*. At least in part she learned this by watching Austen write novels about the social and political divisions of another wartime age, set them in country houses of rural England, and give them titles like *Sense and Sensibility*. For both writers, novels do not just reflect history, which ironically they are often taken to eschew; they write history through the histories of women's lives.

Select Bibliography

Armstrong, Nancy. *Desire and Domestic Fiction: A political history of the novel.* New York and Oxford: Oxford University Press, 1987. A provocative study of the construction of sexuality in fictional and non-fictional texts.

Austen, Jane. *Jane Austen's Letters to Her Sister Cassandra and Others.* Edited by R. W. Chapman. 2nd edn. London: Oxford University Press, 1952. The standard source for Austen's correspondence, superbly annotated and indexed.

Austen, Jane. *The Novels of Jane Austen.* Edited by R. W. Chapman. 5 vols. 3rd edn. London: Oxford University Press, 1932–4. The standard scholarly edition, cited by volume number throughout this study.

Austen, Jane. *Minor Works.* Edited by R. W. Chapman. Vol. VI of *Novels of Jane Austen.* London: Oxford University Press, 1954. Cited in this study as Volume 6 of the novels.

Austen, Jane. *Sense and Sensibility.* Edited by Tony Tanner. Harmondsworth: Penguin, 1969. Long the standard teaching edition of the novel, with an interesting introduction.

Austen, Jane. *Sense and Sensibility.* Edited by Margaret Doody. London: Oxford World's Classics, 1990. Should supplant Tanner's as the standard classroom edition; superb introduction.

Austen, Henry. 'Biographical notice of the author'. Reprinted in the Penguin edition of *Northanger Abbey*, ed. Anne Henry Ehrenpreis (Harmondsworth, 1972).

Austen-Leigh, James Edward. *A Memoir of Jane Austen.* London: Richard Bentley, 1870. Reprinted in the Penguin edition of *Persuasion*, ed. D. W. Harding (Harmondsworth, 1965).

Babb, Howard. *Jane Austen's Novels: The fabric of dialogue.* Columbus, OH: Ohio State University Press, 1962. An early but detailed and sophisticated study of Austen's style.

Bloom, Harold, ed. *Modern Critical Views: Jane Austen.* New York: Chelsea House, 1986. The strongest collection of recent essays on Austen's fiction.

Select Bibliography

Booth, Wayne. *The Rhetoric of Fiction*. 2nd. edn. Chicago, IL: University of Chicago Press, 1983. Important study of fictional aesthetics, with significant treatment of Austen.

Bradbrook, Frank W. *Jane Austen and Her Predecessors*. Cambridge: Cambridge University Press, 1967. Remains the standard work on literary influences on Austen.

Brown, Julia Prewitt. *A Reader's Guide to the Nineteenth-Century English Novel*. New York: Macmillan, 1985. A mine of information about such social concerns as money, class, education and religion.

Burke, Edmund. *Reflections on the Revolution in France*. Garden City, NY: Doubleday, 1973.

Burney, Fanny. *Evelina*. Edited by Edward A. Bloom with Lillian D. Bloom. Oxford and New York: Oxford University Press, 1982.

Butler, Marilyn. *Jane Austen and the War of Ideas*. Oxford: Oxford University Press, 1975. A richly detailed presentation of Austen as an anti-Jacobin spokesman for the conservative interest.

Butler, Marilyn. *Romantics, Rebels, and Reactionaries*. New York: Oxford University Press, 1982. A social history of literature of the romantic period, accessible to the general reader.

Chandler, James K. *Wordsworth's Second Nature: A study of the poetry and politics*. Chicago, IL: University of Chicago Press, 1984. Outstanding and influential study of the influence of Burke on the most important poet of Austen's generation.

Duckworth, Alistair. *The Improvement of the Estate*. Baltimore, MD: Johns Hopkins University Press, 1971. The first major study of Austen as a conservative social thinker; less historical detail than Butler's *War*, but richer readings of the novels.

English, Barbara and Saville, John. *Strict Settlement: A guide for historians*. Occasional Papers in Economic and Social History, No. 10. Hull: University of Hull Press, 1983. A concise guide to English inheritance law.

Evans, Mary. *Jane Austen and the State*. London and New York: Tavistock, 1987. A provocative essay presenting Austen as a radical critic of bourgeois capitalism.

Fergus, Jan. *Jane Austen and the Didactic Novel:* Northanger Abbey, Sense and Sensibility, *and* Pride and Prejudice. Totowa, NJ: Barnes and Noble, 1983. Subtle and detailed readings of the rhetorical structures of Austen's early novels.

Fleishman, Avrom. *A Reading of* Mansfield Park. Minneapolis, MN: University of Minnesota Press, 1967. Landmark exploration of this novel in its intellectual, social and cultural context.

Gaull, Marilyn. *English Romanticism: The human context*. New

York: Norton, 1988. An excellent source-book for students on the writers, movements, forms and personalities of the period.

Gilbert, Sandra and Gubar, Susan. *The Madwoman in the Attic*. New Haven, CT: Yale University Press, 1979. The chapters on Austen present her as a subtle critic of the patriarchal establishment.

Gilson, David. *A Bibliography of Jane Austen*. Oxford: Clarendon Press, 1982. A monumental work recording and describing the early editions of the novels, translations, subsequent editions, letters, dramatisations, continuations and completions, books owned by Austen, and biography and criticism up to 1978.

Godwin, William. *Enquiry Concerning Political Justice and Its Influence on Morals and Happiness*. Edited by F. E. T. Priestley. Toronto: University of Toronto Press, 1967.

Grey, J. David, *et. al. The Jane Austen Companion*. New York: Macmillan, 1986. An excellent compilation of brief essays on Austenian topics with a chronology of her life and works.

Halperin, John, ed. *Jane Austen: Bicentenary essays*. Cambridge: Cambridge University Press, 1975. An excellent collection of original essays for the bicentenary of Austen's birth.

Halperin, John, ed. *The Life of Jane Austen*. Sussex: Harvester Wheatsheaf, 1984. A controversial biography, with more in common with the 'subversive' school of Austen criticism than is customary among her biographers.

Handler, Richard and Segal, Daniel. *Jane Austen and the Fiction of Culture*. Tucson, AZ: University of Arizona Press, 1990. An intriguing approach to Austen's novels through methods derived from anthropological study.

Hardy, Barbara. *A Reading of Jane Austen*. New York: New York University Press, 1976. A topical study attending to Austen's contributions to the art of the novel.

Hewitt, Regina. *Wordsworth and the Empirical Dilemma*. New York: Peter Lang, 1990.

Hodge, Jane Aiken. *The Double Life of Jane Austen*. London: Hodder and Stoughton, 1972.

Hodge, Jane Aiken. 'Jane Austen and her publishers'. In *Jane Austen: Bicentenary essays*, ed. Halperin, 75–85.

Honan, Park. *Jane Austen: Her life*. London: Weidenfeld & Nicolson, 1987. Readable and reliable, the standard biography to date.

Jenkins, Elizabeth. *Jane Austen: A biography*. London: Victor Gollancz, 1938.

Johnson, Claudia L. *Jane Austen: Women, politics, and the novel*. Chicago, IL: University of Chicago Press, 1988. A richly contextualised study of Austen's affinities with progressive, reformist social thought; one of those rare works which combines firm

117

historical understanding with persuasive, elegant, sophisticated readings of the novels.

Johnson, Claudia L. 'The "Twilight of Probability": uncertainty and hope in *Sense and Sensibility*'. *Philological Quarterly*, 62 (1983), 171–86.

Kay, Carol. *Political Constructions: Defoe, Richardson, and Sterne in relation to Hobbes, Hume, and Burke*. Ithaca, NY: Cornell University Press, 1988. Extremely interesting treatment of Edmund Burke's impact on British philosophical and literary culture.

Kestner, Joseph. 'Jane Austen: the tradition of the English Romantic novel, 1800–1832'. *Wordsworth Circle*, 7 (1976), 297–311.

Kirkham, Margaret. *Jane Austen, Feminism, and Fiction*. Sussex: Harvester Wheatsheaf, 1983. A study of Austen's sympathy with the 'rational feminism of the Enlightment'.

Kroeber, Karl. *Styles in Fictional Structure: The art of Jane Austen, Charlotte Brontë, George Eliot*. Princeton, NJ: Princeton University Press, 1971. Pioneering effort in comparative stylistics based on quantitative methods.

Lascelles, Mary. *Jane Austen and Her Art*. Oxford: Oxford University Press, 1939. Remains a useful and readable overview of Austen's life and art.

Litz, A. Walton. *Jane Austen: A study of her artistic development*. New York: Oxford University Press, 1965. Another classic study, with intelligent and sensitive readings of the works.

McGann, Jerome J. *The Romantic Ideology*. Chicago, IL: University of Chicago Press, 1983. Influential new historicist manifesto which addresses the issue of Austen's romanticism, or lack of it.

Miller, D. A. *Narrative and Its Discontents: Problems of closure in the traditional novel*. Princeton, NJ: Princeton University Press, 1981. A sophisticated study of fictional form in Austen, Eliot and Stendhal.

Monaghan, David. *Jane Austen: Structure and social vision*. London: Macmillan, 1980. A close analysis of the role of 'social rituals' in Austen's fiction.

Morgan, Susan. *In the Meantime: Character and perception in Jane Austen's fiction*. Chicago, IL: University of Chicago Press, 1980. A beautifully written study, offering an Austen who is far more romantic, with stronger affinities with the romantic poets, than is commonly realised.

Mudrick, Marvin. *Jane Austen: Irony as defense and discovery*. Princeton, NJ: Princeton University Press, 1952. An influential study of the 'subversive' Austen, concentrating on the complexity and power of her ironic vision and method.

Select Bibliography

Page, Norman. *The Language of Jane Austen.* Oxford: Basil Blackwell, 1972. Solid and interesting stylistic analysis, which shows that Austen's prose 'exhibits a much greater degree of stylistic variety than is sometimes supposed'.

Paine, Thomas. *The Rights of Man.* In Burke, Edmund. *Reflections on the Revolution in France.* Garden City, NY: Doubleday, 1973.

Pocock, J. G. A. *Politics, Language and Time.* New York: Atheneum, 1971.

Poovey, Mary. *The Proper Lady and the Woman Writer.* Chicago, IL: University of Chicago Press, 1984. Treats Austen's career in the context provided by Wollstonecraft's and Mary Shelley's telling observations on the tension between support for the authority of traditional institutions and the attractions of individualism.

Roberts, Warren. *Jane Austen and the French Revolution.* New York: St Martin's, 1979. Largely historical study of 'how the Revolution entered Austen's world and affected her writing and thinking'.

Roth, Barry. *An Annotated Bibliography of Jane Austen Studies, 1973–1983.* Charlottesville, VA: University of Virginia Press, 1985.

Ruoff, Gene W. '1800 and the future of the novel: William Wordsworth, Maria Edgeworth, and the vagaries of literary history'. In *The Age of William Wordsworth: Critical essays on the romantic tradition*, eds Kenneth R. Johnston and Gene Ruoff. New Brunswick, NJ: Rutgers University Press, 1987, pp. 291–314.

Ruoff, Gene W. 'Anne Elliot's dowry: reflections on the ending of *Persuasion*'. *The Wordsworth Circle*, 7 (1976), 342–51.

Ruoff, Gene W. 'The sense of a beginning: Mansfield Park and romantic narrative'. *The Wordsworth Circle*, 10 (1979), 174–86.

Ruoff, Gene W. 'The triumph of *Persuasion*: Jane Austen and the creation of woman'. *Persuasions*, 6 (1984), 54–61.

Scott, P. J. M. *Jane Austen: A reassessment.* Totowa, NJ: Barnes & Noble, 1982. Includes a strong appreciation of *Sense and Sensibility*'s tragic vision of lost human potential.

Sedgwick, Eve Kosofsky. 'Jane Austen and the masturbating girl'. *Critical Inquiry*, 17 (1991), 819–37. An essay, which became famous before its publication, attempting to define the nature of sexuality in *Sense and Sensibility*.

Siskin, Clifford. *The Historicity of Romantic Discourse.* New York: Oxford University Press, 1988. Includes interesting analysis of the historical problems involved in linking Austen to other writers of her age.

Southam, B. C., ed. *Jane Austen: The critical heritage.* London: Routledge & Kegan Paul, 1968. The standard compendium of commentary on Austen up to 1870, with an excellent introduction. Cited as *CH1*.

Southam, B. C., ed. *Jane Austen: The critical heritage, 1870–1940.* Volume 2. London and New York: Routledge & Kegan Paul, 1987. Continuation of the above, 1870–1940. Cited as *CH2*.

Southam, B. C., ed. *Jane Austen:* Sense and Sensibility, Pride and Prejudice, *and* Mansfield Park. London: Macmillan, 1976. A casebook gathering classic treatments of the three novels.

Stone, Lawrence. *The Family, Sex and Marriage in England 1500– 1800.* Abr. edn. New York: Harper & Row, 1979. An outstanding social history of the family in England.

Sulloway, Alison G. *Jane Austen and the Province of Womanhood.* Philadelphia, PA: University of Pennsylvania Press, 1989. Austen as a moderate feminist, presented with strong historical contextualisation.

Swingle, L. J. *The Obstinate Questionings of English Romanticism.* Baton Rouge, LA: Louisiana State University Press, 1987. An elegantly written exploration of romantic scepticism, unusual in that it gives extended consideration to fiction generally and Austen particularly.

Swingle, L. J. 'The perfect happiness of the union: Jane Austen's *Emma*'. *The Wordsworth Circle*, 7 (1976), 312–19.

Swingle, L. J. 'The poets, the novelists, and the Romantic Situation'. *The Wordsworth Circle*, 10 (1979), 218–28.

Tanner, Tony. *Jane Austen.* Cambridge, MA: Harvard University Press, 1986. Collects revised versions of Tanner's graceful and interesting introductions to three Penguin editions, including *Sense and Sensibility*, with his more recent writings on Austen.

Tave, Stuart. *Some Words of Jane Austen.* Chicago, IL: University of Chicago Press, 1973. A major study of Austen's art, with meticulous and compelling readings of the works.

Thompson, James. *Between Self and World: The novels of Jane Austen.* University Park, PA: Pennsylvania State University Press, 1988. An attentive Lukácsian study of Austen's novels, proceeding according to social/historical topics. Major attention to *Sense and Sensibility* is in a chapter entitled 'Courtship, marriage, and work'.

Tucker, George Holbert. *A Goodly Heritage: A history of Jane Austen's family.* Manchester: Carcanet Press, 1983. Especially useful on the Warren Hastings circle.

Watt, Ian. *The Rise of the Novel.* Berkeley, CA: University of California Press, 1957. Standard study of the emergence of the social novel in England.

Wiesenfarth, Joseph. *The Errand of Form: An essay on Jane Austen's*

Art. New York: Fordham University Press, 1967. Focuses on 'problems' in the novels; the chapter on *Sense and Sensibility* provides an intelligent reconsideration of the role of Colonel Brandon.

Wollstonecraft, Mary. *A Vindication of the Rights of Woman.* Edited by Miriam Brody Kramnick. Harmondsworth: Penguin, 1982.

Woolf, Virginia. *The Common Reader.* San Diego, CA: Harcourt, Brace & Jovanovich, 1984. Superb chapter entitled 'Jane Austen' and a perennially fresh and relevant chapter entitled 'Modern fiction'.

Wright, Andrew. *Jane Austen's Novels: A study in structure.* New York: Oxford University Press, 1953. An early but still useful examination of aspects of Austen's art; very good on management of point of view.

Index

Index